MARRIAGE
AS A
RELATIONSHIP

MARRIAGE
AS A
RELATIONSHIP
Real and Rational

Margaret Monahan Hogan

Afterword by Sidney Callahan

MARQUETTE
UNIVERSITY
PRESS

Marquette Studies in Philosophy
No. 34
Andrew Tallon, Series Editor

Library of Congress Cataloguing-in-Publication Data
Hogan, Margaret Monahan.
Marriage as a relationship : real and rational / Margaret Monahan
Hogan ; afterword by Sidney Callahan.— New ed., rev. and corrected.
p. cm. — (Marquette studies in philosophy ; #34)
Rev. ed. of: Finality and marriage. 1993.
Includes bibliographical references and index.
ISBN 0-87462-657-9 (pbk. : alk. paper)
1. Marriage—Religious aspects—Catholic Church. 2. Catholic
Church—Doctrines. I. Hogan, Margaret Monahan. Finality and
marriage. II. Title. III. Series.
BX2250 .H62 2002
241'.63—dc21

2002152482

New Edition, Revised and Corrected,
of *Finality and Marriage* (1993),
with a new title, cover, ISBN, series number,
Preface, Index, Fourth Chapter
—responding to questions raised by the first edition—
and a new Afterword by Sidney Callahan.

Cover: Gerard ter Borch II, *The Suitor's Visit,*
Andrew W. Mellon Collection, Photograph © 2002 Board of Trustees,
National Gallery of Art, Washington, c. 1658,
oil on canvas, .800 x .750 (32 1/2 x 29 9/16), detail.

Table of Contents

Chapter 3

Chapter 4

In memory of my parents

Mr. and Mrs. Edward J. Monahan

... who have gone ahead to prepare for our coming.

Preface

This work is an exploration of moral philosophy within the ethical institution of Roman Catholicism regarding its position on: (1) the essential nature of marriage, (2) the several finalities to be accomplished within marriage, (3) the role of conjugal intercourse, and (4) the governance of the reproductive finality within marriage. This work attempts to contribute to that ongoing discussion with an examination of the position of the tradition as enunciated in the documents of the tradition. It begins with a study of the documents of the immediate past. These documents are *Casti Connubii* and the *Allocutions* of Pope Pius XII. It continues with an examination of the position of the tradition as found in the documents of the present. These documents are *Gaudium et spes, Humanae vitae,* and *Donum vitae.* The work then delineates an emerging position regarding the essential nature of marriage, the role of conjugal intercourse as the sign which signifies and contains the reality that is marriage, the ordering of the several finalities to be accomplished in marriage, and the implications of this position on the regulation of reproduction. The account of the emergent position provides the framework for the examination of significant contemporary positions within the tradition and a framework for resolving conflicts among the ends to be accomplished within marriage. Finally, the work concludes with responses to three major sets of questions, the first on the possibility of the development of doctrine, the second on the possibility of homosexual marriage, and the third on the application of the theoretical position to the practice of living the morally good marriage, from within the context of the emergent position.

In this new profile, marriage is characterized as a special kind of human relationship. It is an intimate personal union which is to supply the matrix of conditions for the perfection of the marriage, for procreation, and for the perfection of the partners. Marriage has three ends:

(1) personal union — intrinsic necessary end
(2) procreation — intrinsic contingent end
(3) personalist — intrinsic contingent end.

These ends press for actualization on three distinct interrelated levels: horizontal, vertical, and transcendental. Governance of the reproductive finality is directed from within the marital matrix.

It is not the intention of this small work to serve as a catalogue of the extensive secondary literature on marriage and its ends. References to the secondary literature abound in larger tomes familiar to all who study the question of marriage in the Catholic tradition. It is not the intention of this work to engage all contemporary commentators on marriage. Its dialogue is limited to a sampling of those who hold important opposing views. It is not the intention of this work to approach such vexing questions, as that of the role of the scholar within the tradition, that are besetting contemporary Catholicism. The task of this work is to locate, in a carefully delineated account of the nature of marriage, that higher point of view—the *Aufhebung*, under which the opposing viewpoints may be seen as partial viewpoints and within which meaningful conversation may begin among the well intentioned and scholarly people on all sides of the issue.

The conclusion of a book marks the occasion for an author to look back with thanks to all who made the work possible. As a wife and mother, gratitude must first be extended to my husband, Dr. Thomas P. Hogan and my children, Mary Teresa, Thomas, Jr., Edward, Daniel, Matthew, and Meg for their encouragement, their patient understanding, and their joy in the completion of this work. As a daughter, gratitude must be extended to my parents, Mr. and Mrs. Edward J. Monahan, who considered the education of a daughter just as important as the education of a son and whose life together provided my first glimpse of the reality of the unity of marriage. They have now gone on to that joyous union with God that our faith promises. Their wish, which echoes that attributed to Thomas More, that we may one day merrily meet in heaven, remains the hope of their children and grandchildren. As a scholar, gratitude must be extended to those who nurtured that scholarship. I have been privileged to have been taught by men and women, both in the classroom and in their works, whom

I continue to regard as giants in their fields. They include Dr. Andrew
Tallon, Dr. Patrick Coffey, and Dr. Keith Algozin who were my men-
tors at Marquette University. Without their competent teaching, and
their gentle, cheerful encouragement, this work would never have been
brought to completion. To them, of course, goes none of the blame
for any failure on my part to "get it right." I remain most grateful
to Fr. Richard McCormick, S.J., and Dr. Sidney Callahan for their
contributions to this text. Fr. McCormick wrote the original *Foreword*
and remained steadfast in his support and in his interest in my work
in this field. In January 2000, shortly before his death, he completed
his promise to get a copy of his final paper on marriage, presented to
the Catholic Theological Society of America, to me before his papers
were sealed. Dr. Callahan, despite a very busy and demanding profes-
sional and personal schedule, consented to contribute the *Afterword*.
I am indebted to King's College and the University of Notre Dame,
especially the Notre Dame Center for Ethics and Culture and Dr.
David Solomon, for their support that allowed the completion of this
text. My thanks to Dr. Patricia McAdams, Fr. Mark Poorman, and
Sr. Patricia Dearbaugh, I.H.M., and the women of Cavanaugh for
their hospitality at Notre Dame during the year I spent in residence
there. I am especially indebted to Ms. Elizabeth Didgeon, Ms. Donna
Kazmierski, and Mrs. Joan Francis, faculty assistants at King's College,
for their patience in the preparation of this text.

Foreword

to the First Edition

Richard A. McCormick, S.J.

Finality and Marriage is a book about the nature of marriage, its ends and its act. Philosopher Margaret Monahan Hogan is convinced that only when we accurately grasp the *vetera* (the essential elements of the tradition) will be prepared to move to the *nova*. This move is a continuity. For this reason Hogan examines the notion of marriage and its ends in the documents of recent tradition beginning with *Casti connubii*. Hogan is no iconoclast. Her treatment is full, fair and respectful.

She notes that in the last sixty years there has been a gradual but perceptible development in official documents. What was suspect in the thirties (e.g., Herbert Doms' *Vom Sinn und Zweck der Ehe*) is contemporary orthodoxy. Concretely, Hogan traces the conceptual move of Church documents from marriage as a procreative institution to marriage as an intimate personal union. It is within this notion of marriage that we must weigh the distinct ends of marriage (the union itself, children, and the individual goods of the partners) hierarchize them and articulate the claims they make upon us.

Hogan finds the demand of inseparability for the unitive and procreative aspects of every act of sexual intercourse to be without foundation (p. 96). She takes the consequences of this (pp. 139-140) when she finds contraception (and even sterilization) and artificial insemination morally appropriate given sufficient reason. But these matters are not highlighted.

Indeed, if one is going to disagree with Hogan's conclusions, one must wrestle with their suppositions about the nature of marriage and its ends. For it is from these more basic analyses that her conclusions flow. And herein lies the value and distinct contribution of this study. It starts with basic concerns, not with conclusions to defend or destroy.

In this the study resembles the work of Bernard Lonergan upon whom Hogan obviously relies. We know what Lonergan thought of *Humanae vitae*'s conclusion. In his words: 'no valid reason whatever for a precept.' His analysis is published in the *Lonergan Studies Newsletter*, specifically in the understanding of marriage supposed in concrete conclusions and the method that leads to such understanding. He told me this on several occasions.

Introduction

Moral philosophy within the ethical institution that is Roman Catholicism has witnessed and is witnessing, with increasing intransigence, the debate regarding the very meaning as well as the appropriate means of accomplishing the Biblical injunction, "Be fruitful and multiply; fill the earth and subdue it" (Gn 1:27-28) and the Biblical injunction, "For this reason a man leaves his father and mother and clings to his wife, and the two shall become one flesh" (Gn 2:18, 22-24). The issues within the debate include (1) the delineation of the essential nature of marriage, (2) the specification and valuation of the ends of marriage, and (3) the examination of the implications in regard to the regulation of the accomplishment or avoidance of the reproductive finality brought about by the transition in the understanding of the nature of marriage and the ends of marriage. The debate continues within a matrix that is marked by the presence in modern society of a variety of pressures including the affirmation of the dignity of women as full participants in the progressive enterprise of human existence, the advances in the sciences as they relate to humanity, and the increasing demands on the resources of families to educate children to be contributing members, as people called to union with God.

This work attempts to contribute to that ongoing discussion with an examination of the position of the tradition as enunciated in the documents of the tradition. It begins with a study of the documents of the immediate past. These documents are *Casti connubii* and the allocutions of Pope Pius XII. It continues with an examination of the position of the tradition as found in the documents of the present. These documents are *Gaudium et spes, Humanae vitae,* and *The Instruction on Respect for Human Life in its Origin and on the Dignity of Procreation.* (Hereinafter this document will be referred to as *Donum vitae*). The work, then, attempts to delineate an emerging position regarding the essential nature of marriage, the ordering of the several finalities to be accomplished in marriage, and the implications of this position on the regulation of reproduction. The account of the emergent position provides the framework for the examination of significant contemporary interpretations from within the tradition, both counterpositions and complementary positions, as well as a framework for the evaluation of the position of the tradition itself.

In Chapter One, the position of the tradition as found in the documents of the immediate past is presented. The documents that are examined are *Casti connubii* and the allocutions of Pope Pius XII. The encyclical *Casti connubii* contains a summary of the teachings of the past regarding the nature of marriage and the accomplishment of the ends of marriage. Furthermore, the encyclical provides the foundation for the documents of the present. *Casti connubii* maintains that the essential nature of marriage is a procreative institution. Conjugal intercourse, the act which signifies and contains the reality that is marriage, is primarily a procreative act. Other goods, secondary ends such as remediation of concupiscence and mutual aid, may be accomplished within the conjugal act. However, there may be no direct interference with the accomplishment of the primary end. The nature of marriage as an intimate union and the role of conjugal intercourse in the service of the union appear only in inchoate form in *Casti connubii*. Furthermore, the resolution of problems regarding the accomplishment of the various ends of marriage is effectuated by reference to marriage as, essentially, a procreative institution.

Next, the allocutions of Pope Pius XII, which address the nature and ends of marriage, birth and conception regulation, and surgical procedures related to the reproductive finality, are examined. While these addresses do not have the same status as an encyclical or a conciliar document, they did provide the norms that controlled the resolution of contemporaneous questions related to the several finalities within marriage. The earlier allocutions of Pope Pius XII contain an understanding of the nature of marriage as a procreative institution that is similar to the understanding of the essential nature of marriage found in *Casti connubii*. However, in the later allocutions, especially those dealing with the question of artificial insemination, a new understanding of the nature of marriage begins to appear. In this understanding, marriage begins to be considered a procreative union. Conjugal intercourse, as the act which signifies the reality of marriage, is both a procreative act and a unitive act. And procreation outside the union is proscribed.

In Chapter Two, the position as found in the most recent three documents developing the tradition is made explicit. These documents are *Gaudium et spes, Humanae vitae,* and *Donum vitae.* In addition to the explication of the nature of marriage, the ordering of the several finalities to be accomplished within marriage, and the implications of this ordering for the regulation of reproduction, some important topics to be explored are isolated. Among these are the following: (1) the foundation of the position, (2) the symmetry of argumentation, and (3) the philosophical principles underlying the argumentation. In regard to the foundation of the position of the documents, two important notions are (a) the natural law foundation with the difference in meaning that results from different interpretations of natural law and (b) the claim that the foundation of the position is the dignity of the person as opposed to the counterclaim that the foundation of the position is the biological constitution of the human being. In regard to the symmetry of the argumentation in the documents the concern is that the same principles be applied consistently to the several ends, namely, the unitive, the procreative, and the personalist, to be accomplished in marriage. In regard to the philosophical principles in the documents of the position of the tradition several important principles and determinations are operative including (a) the principle of double effect with the direct/indirect distinction in the application of the principle and the shift from the direct/indirect distinction to the notion of sufficient proportionate reason as controlling in the application of the principle, (b) the principle of totality and the application of that principle to the whole course of marriage rather than to single acts within the marriage as well as the application of that principle to the generative process considered as one power of the person, and (c) the question of the determination of the intrinsic evil in an action.

In Chapter Three, a new position is presented. The delineation of the emergent position unfolds with the exposition of the transition, in the twentieth century, in the specification of the nature of marriage that was accompanied by a corresponding transition in the understanding of the role of conjugal intercourse. It continues with a new profile of the nature of marriage and the delineation of a correspondingly appropriate role of conjugal intercourse. In this new profile marriage is characterized as a special kind of human relationship. It is, essentially, an intimate personal union which is to supply the matrix of conditions for procreation and the perfection of the partners of the union. Marriage, then, has three ends: (1) the personal union, (2) children, and (3) the flourishing of the individual persons, whose actualization brings about the perfection of the marriage. These ends press for actualization on three distinct but interrelated levels. The result is three sets of ends of marriage, the unitive, the procreative, and the personalist, each operative on three distinct but related levels: (1) the level of horizontal finality, (2) the level of vertical finality, and (3) the level of transcendental finality. Horizontal finality is the reference of each thing to its commensurate motives and ends. Vertical finality is marked by the upthrust from lower to higher levels of appetition. Transcendental finality is the reference of all things to God. The development of the ends of marriage on these three levels derives from the ethical theory developed and continuous from Aristotle to Thomas Aquinas to contemporary ethicians, including Bernard Lonergan. The unitive end as the relation between the partners on the level of horizontal finality pursues satisfaction of appetitive, passional inclinations of the organisms, on the vertical level the upward dispositive striving is toward friendship, the deliberate friendship of reason, and on the transcendental level the finality is from friendship to charity. The procreative end as the accomplishment of children on the horizontal level tends to the existence of children, on the vertical directs the education of children as members of the family and the community, and on the level of transcendental finality aspires to the eternal salvation of children. The personalist end as the development and actualization of the individual on the level of horizontal finality pursues life, on the level of vertical finality the good life, on the level of transcendental finality eternal life.

Chapter Three continues with the delineation of support for the appropriateness of this characterization of marriage as essentially a union as found in the Scriptures, in the insights of the philosophy that is foundational for the tradition, in the most recent documents of the tradition, and in contemporary commentary within the tradition. The purpose of this explicitation is to exhibit the historically conditioned elements in the understanding of marriage and to isolate from these the permanent elements of the heritage, especially the notion of marriage as a union. To attempt to accomplish this task is to do what Bernard Lonergan described in the "Epilogue" of *Insight* in regard to the recovery of Thomism in Lonergan's historical studies, *Gratia operans* and *Verbum*. He says of his work of the application of critical intelligence to the understanding of the tradition that it enabled him to "grasp what . . . the *vetera* really were, but also it opened challenging vistas on what the *nova* could be" (Lonergan 1964, 748). The work of this section, then, is to locate the essential elements of the tradition, what Lonergan calls the *vetera* that are to be carried forward to constitute the *nova* that are adequate to meet the exigencies of the contemporary world.

This is followed in the final section of Chapter Three by the consideration of the consequences of (1) this more complete account of the nature of marriage, (2) the sets of ends to be accomplished in marriage, and (3) the appropriate role of conjugal intercourse on the governance of the reproductive finality. Marriage is, in its essential nature, an intimate personal union. This intimate personal union supplies the matrix of conditions in which children should flourish and the partners of the marriage should flourish. Conjugal intercourse is the marriage act. As expressive of the reality of marriage it must always signify the marital union. Conjugal intercourse is appropriate to nourish and sustain the marital union. Conjugal intercourse is appropriate within marriage to realize the end which is the good of children. The good of children may be sought in marriage under the conditions of reasonableness and responsibility. Furthermore, conjugal intercourse is appropriate within marriage to satisfy the individual needs of the partners. These individual goods may be sought in marriage under the governance of chastity and friendship.

The variance of these conclusions from the conclusions of the documents of the tradition in the twentieth century is not to be viewed as a disagreement with the tradition but rather a development of the tradition in the presence of a more complete understanding of the nature of marriage. This more complete understanding of the nature of marriage, its ends, and its act is the product of a methodology that examines the content of the sacred tradition within a changed horizon, a horizon that has expanded beyond classical, object-limited inquiry to a horizon defined as the contemporary cultural context. That contemporary cultural context is an historicist context that is the result of the critical revolution in philosophy and the empirical revolution in science, including philosophy as scientific. The critical revolution in philosophy is marked by the shift from performative but unthematized interiority to explicitly critical interiority with the resultant emphasis on the contribution of subjectivity and reason to law. The empirical revolution in science, which retains the theoretic exigence which characterized the classical sciences, is marked by a transition in the ideal of science and a new conception of science itself. The characteristics that mark the qualitative shift from a classicist context to an historicist context are several and are described by Lonergan in various works including *Dimensions of Meaning*. In summary, the transition may be described in the following series of shifts: (1) from certainty of results to probability of results, (2) from attention to the changeless and immobile to concern with change, movement, and development, (3) from emphasis on the role of the universal and necessary judgment in knowledge to emphasis on the role of the judgment of fact as the incremental factor in knowledge, (4) from exclusive concentration on the universal to controlling interest accorded all phenomena—the concrete, the particular, the contingent facts in their mutually intelligible relationships, (5) from pursuit of science as a matter of logic to the pursuit of science as a matter of method, (6) from the notion of science as a permanent achievement to the notion of science as an open developing process, (7) from science as individual—the habit of the scientist—to science as a work of collaboration in the scientific community. (Lonergan 1967a, 252ff.).

Chapter 4, an extended Epilogue, responds to particular questions and critical comments that have been raised and offered since the first publication of the text. For the most part comments have been favorable, but the critical comments and questions put forth by serious scholars require careful attention. These latter fall into three categories: (A) the work is incorrect and it represents a serious departure from the Catholic teaching on marriage; (B) the work is correct as far as it goes, but is incomplete, that is, it does not address the possibility of same sex marriage; and (C) the work is correct but incomplete, that is, it fails to apply the theoretical in any practical way that is useful for married couples. The Epilogue responds, separately and briefly, to each of those questions.

Chapter 1

The Past:
The Recovery of the Tradition

The latter half of the twentieth century witnessed the promulgation of three major documents which focus attention on and develop the tradition within Roman Catholicism regarding the nature of marriage and the accomplishment of the ends of marriage. These documents are *Gaudium et spes, Humanae vitae*, and *Donum vitae*. They were immediately preceded in this contemporary era by the encyclical *Casti connubii* of Pope Pius XI and several allocutions of Pope Pius XII, which, while continuous with the many major elements in the understanding of the tradition on marriage, represent also the response of the tradition to the problems of the contemporaneous society and, hence, development of the tradition. To place the more recent documents in proper context in regard to the tradition, an elucidation of these core notions from *Casti connubii,* constituting a summation of the essential elements of the tradition, and from the Papal allocutions seems appropriate.

Pope Pius XI: *Casti connubii*

Introduction

The encyclical *Casti connubii* was issued on December 31, 1930. It was presented against a background which included religious, intellectual, pastoral, and sociological pressures some of which were inimical, some of which were challenging, and some of which were enhancements of elements of the tradition. This background has been amply described by John Noonan in his work *Contraception:*

A History of its Treatment by the Catholic Theologians and Canonists.
The delineation of the opposing challenges may serve to bring the
direction of the encyclical into sharper focus. The opposing religious
pressures that were brought to bear include those within Christianity
and within Catholicism. Included in the religious pressures within
Christianity, but outside the confines of the institution of Roman
Catholicism, was the action of the Lambeth Conference of August
14, 1930 which sanctioned the practice of contraception within marriage whenever there was a serious reason to exclude the possibility of
additional children. The resolution states,

> Where there is a clearly felt moral obligation to limit or avoid
> parenthood, the method must be decided on Christian principles.
> The primary and obvious method is complete abstinence from
> intercourse (as far as may be necessary) in a life of discipline and
> self-control lived in the power of the Holy Spirit. Nevertheless in
> those cases where there is such a clearly-felt moral obligation to
> limit or avoid parenthood, and where there is a morally sound
> reason for avoiding complete abstinence, the conference agrees that
> other methods may be used, provided this is done in the light of
> the same Christian principles. The Conference records its strong
> condemnation of the use of any methods of conception control from
> motives of selfishness, luxury, or mere convenience. (The Lambeth
> Conference, 1930, Resolution 15; in Noonan 1986, 409.)

Heretofore, various Lambeth Conferences had adopted resolutions
containing absolute prohibitions of contraception.

Within the confines of its own theological circles, Roman Catholicism witnessed uneasiness as evidenced in the representative article of
Matthias Laros "Revolutionierung der Ehe" in the German periodical
Hochland in June, 1930. The article of Laros raised questions about
the natural law foundation of the Catholic position on the ends of
marriage. His specific questions, which persist in the contemporary
era, include (1) whether the prohibition of contraception is an absolute
prohibition, (2) what does natural law command in a conflict among
the various goods of marriage, namely, peace in the family, education
of children, and procreation of children, and (3) what is meant by

the characterization of contraception as unlawful and intrinsically evil (Laros 1930, 193-207, in Noonan 1986, 425).

The pressures on the pastoral level were fueled by the uneasy, and not unfounded, suspicion that parish priests, in the presence of their own doubts and uncertainties, were neither teaching nor enforcing the teaching of the tradition by way of appropriate confessional interrogation. In addition, in secular intellectual circles many scientists, academics, and physicians, as evidenced by resolutions and publications of various learned societies, shifted from the view that held contraception as morally dangerous and medically unhealthy to views that ranged from the guarded acceptance of contraception in appropriate pressing circumstances to enthusiastic espousal of contraception as a tool to rid the world of various social evils. The latter notion was carried by the national and international groups espousing population control. In society as a whole, the problems of abortion, of forced sterilization, of marriages of Catholics with those of other religions, of divorce, as well as that of the emancipation of women complete the mosaic of the societal background that occasioned the proclamation of Pope Pius XI.

Marriage: Nature and Ends

In the presence of these pressures, *Casti connubii* affirmed certain truths regarding the nature, the ends, and the benefits of marriage in opposition to the errors of the day. It has been said of *Casti connubii* that it represents a synthesis of the tradition in which the following themes are present: "the Hebrew emphasis on procreation, the antignostic teaching of Timothy, the Augustinian doctrine of the marital goods, the Thomistic view of the nature of the coital act, the nineteenth-century theology on the sin of Onan" (Noonan 1986, 427). *Casti connubii* sets down the following as true regarding the nature of marriage: marriage is a divine institution; marriage is a sacrament; and marriage is an intimate union. The document says that it is a "divine institution" (Pius XI 1941, 1) and that from God "comes the very institution of marriage, the ends for which it was instituted, the laws that govern it, the blessings that flow from it" (ibid., 9). What is being affirmed here is that marriage has a nature of its own. Men and women are at liberty to enter into marriage or enter into marriage with a particular person by a free will decision, but they are not free to define what marriage is.

In regard to marriage as a sacrament the document says, "Christ ... having assumed the nature of fallen man ... ordained it in a special manner as the principle and foundation of domestic society ... raised it to the rank of a truly great sacrament of the New Law" (ibid., 1). To consider marriage as a sacrament is to recognize it as a graced state in which the grace of the sacrament perfects the natural condition of marriage in order to direct the spouses to the attainment of their proper supernatural end. The controlling notion here is that of grace as *"gratia operans."* This Augustinian notion, which was more fully developed by Thomas Aquinas, is that of grace building upon nature and that of nature as properly disposed to the reception of grace. As a consequence of its sacramental character, the marital union realizes particular benefits including the firmness and indissolubility of the union and the sanctification of the husband and wife.

In regard to marriage as an intimate union the document says, "By matrimony ... the souls of the contracting parties are joined and knit together, more directly and more intimately than are their bodies" (ibid., 7). Here, despite the expression in dualistic language, what is being maintained is that marriage involves not only bodily union but the union of two persons brought together by a free, firm, and deliberate act of their wills.

The three goods or ends of marriage: children, fidelity, and the sacrament are enumerated in the encyclical after the fashion of Augustine who in "De bono coniugali" wrote, "The good, therefore, of marriage among all nations and all men is in the cause of generation and in the fidelity of chastity; in the case of the people of God, however, the good is also in the sanctity of the sacrament" (Augustine 1955, 47). In the attainment of the good of children the encyclical casts the parents in the role of cooperators with God in the procreation of life and in the role of faithful followers of the Genesis command, "Increase and multiply, and fill the earth" (Pius XI 1941, 11). The good of children is not here limited to the existence of children, "not only that they should live and fill the earth" (ibid., 12). It includes also their education, that is, that they be directed toward their supernatural end, "that they may be worshippers of God, that they may know Him and love Him and finally enjoy Him forever in heaven" (ibid.). To the parents, then, in cooperation with the Creator falls the task of procreation and the task of education, herein described as religious education. Inasmuch as the work of education is recognized as a process which requires the work of both parents over an extended period of time, marriage as an indissoluble union is seen as the necessary condition that the end, the education of children, be accomplished. This echoes the teaching of Augustine who, as is acknowledged in the text of the encyclical, wrote, "As regards the offspring it is provided that they should be begotten lovingly and educated religiously" (ibid., 17).

In the attainment of the second good, that of conjugal fidelity, marriage is described as the state of affairs in which the spouses come together to form a unity in being. The words of Christ as reported in the documents that issued from Trent are repeated here to describe this ontological transformation. They are, "Christ Our Lord very clearly taught that in this bond two persons only are to be united and joined together when He said: 'Therefore they are no longer two, but one flesh'" (ibid., 20). The mutual love, "the deep attachment of the heart" (ibid., 23) of husband and wife is seen as the foundation for the nurturing of conjugal fidelity. The encyclical says,

> This conjugal faith ... blooms more freely, more beautifully and more nobly, when it is rooted in that more excellent soil, the love of husband and wife which pervades all the duties of married life and holds pride of place in Christian marriage (ibid.).

In their working together in this common enterprise of marriage, as it is found in contemporary Western culture, which was begun in love as attraction and desire, "not in the passing lust of the moment" (ibid.), the spouses approach the perfection of themselves, each other, and the marriage itself. This approach to the life of virtue is one which understands virtue as excellence accomplished through the practice of appropriately similar acts throughout a lifetime. The encyclical described these acts as having their source in love, "love ... which ... does not consist in pleasing words only, but in that deep attachment of the heart which is expressed in action, since love is proved by deeds" (ibid.). This love disposes the spouses to make possible the accomplishment of true love of God and neighbor. In regard to this fulfillment of each other the encyclical says,

> This mutual interior formation of husband and wife, this determined effort to perfect each other, can in a very real sense, as the Roman Catechism teaches, be said to be the primary cause and reason of matrimony, provided matrimony be considered not in the restricted sense as the institution designed for the procreation and education of the child, but in the wider sense as a complete and intimate life partnership and association (ibid., 24).

The two senses of marriage, designated here as the stricter sense and the wider sense, refer, respectively, to the understanding of marriage in the Canon Law of 1917 definition and the definition as found in the Catechism of the Council of Trent. The former regards marriage as a procreative institution and specifies it in Canon 1013.1 in these terms: "The primary end of marriage is the procreation and nurture of children; its secondary end is mutual help and the remedying of concupiscence" (in Mackin 1982, 216). The Catechism of the Council of Trent describes marriage as

> [T]he conjugal and intimate union of man and wife, which is to last during life ... the obligation and tie expressed by the word union alone have the force and nature of marriage. The peculiar character of this union is marked by the word conjugal, distinguishing it from other contracts by which persons unite to promote their common interests (Catechism 226-27, in Mackin 1982, 198).

The understanding of the encyclical in this wider sense indicates that the essential nature of marriage is a special kind of human relationship. The Canon Law restricted sense of marriage as a procreative institution is the specification of marriage by one of the components of marriage. As was the case with the education of children, conjugal fidelity, while promised at the inception of the marriage, is accomplished over a long period of time. The indissolubility of marriage is posited as a requirement for its fulfillment.

The third good of marriage is the sacrament. In designating the sacrament as a good of marriage, an end to be accomplished, as well as an essential component of the nature of marriage, the focus here is upon the graced state of marriage and on the goal of marriage to effectuate a union which aspires to instantiate the perfect union of Christ and the Church. The encyclical adverts to the description of the sacramental character of marriage as a constituting element and as a goal from the work of Robert Bellarmine on matrimony in which he says,

> The sacrament of matrimony can be regarded in two ways: first in the making, and then in its permanent state. For it is a sacrament like to that of the Eucharist, which not only when it is being conferred, but also whilst it remains, is a sacrament; for as long as the married parties are alive, so long is their union a sacrament of Christ and the Church. (*De Controversiis*, tom. *III, De matr.*, controvers. II cap. 6; in Pius XI 1941, 110).

In regard to the first, the encyclical calls marriage, "an efficacious sign of grace" (Pius XI 1941, 31). In regard to the second, the letter of Paul to the Ephesians is recalled in the words, "the marriage of Christians recalls that most perfect union which exists between Christ and the Church ... which union, as long as Christ shall live and the Church through Him, can never be dissolved by any separation" (ibid., 36). The accomplishment of the sacrament of marriage requires as a necessary condition the indissolubility of marriage. So binding is this requirement that even if the good of children cannot be achieved in a particular marriage, the marriage cannot be dissolved in order to have children in another marriage. It is said, "It is wrong to leave a wife that is sterile in order to take another by whom children may be had" (ibid.).

In the delineation of the characteristics of marriage, the encyclical asserts that marriage is a divinely instituted union which received its defining characteristics in its creation and which was given a sacramental character by Christ. The ends to be fulfilled that are specifically listed in the document are the following: *Proles, Fides*, and *Sacramentum*. In regard to children (*Proles*), the goals are the related but different ends of the existence of children and the religious education of children. In regard to fidelity (*Fides*), the essential goodness of marital love is affirmed and the goals are the related but different ends of the chaste physical union of the husband and wife, the affection of husband and wife for each other, the advancement in virtue of both, and the increasing disposition of the spouses toward charity. In regard to the sacrament (*Sacramentum*), the end is the perfection of the natural love of the spouses and their mutual sanctification.

Response to Particular Problems

From within the context of these teachings on the nature and ends of marriage, the encyclical responded to the questions of the day and reached several conclusions that are relevant to the unitive and procreative ends of marriage. In regard to the challenges directed against the unitive end, it affirmed that sexual intercourse is properly limited to the marital union. The exercise of intimate union outside of marriage whether the intention be the fulfillment of the generative power or whether the intention be the fulfillment of the desire for companionship is seen as an act against the good of the union. The marital union is indissoluble even if one of the partners is sterile. The marital union is indissoluble even in the absence of "compatibility of temperament" (ibid., 70). In addition, the good of marital union serves the good of the children inasmuch as the union supplies the appropriate conditions for the nurturing, as religious education, of children. Further, the good of the marital union serves the good of the spouses inasmuch as the union supplies the appropriate conditions for the flourishing of the partners.

In regard to the procreative end, the encyclical addressed the pressing questions of the day that opposed this end, that is, those of abortion, birth control, and sterilization. Abortion as a species of taking human life is clearly distinguished from birth control. However, it is viewed as, sometimes, the consequence of a mentality that excludes children as a good of marriage. In its moral specification abortion is characterized as the direct killing of the innocent.

Birth control, in its objective characterization as an act against the law of God and/or an act against the law of nature, is seen as an act which opposes the procreative end of marriage. In regard to birth control as an act against the law of God, reference is made to the Augustinian understanding of the sin of Onan as a contraceptive act, which God punished by the death of Onan (Gen. 38, 8-10). The understanding of birth control as an act against the law of nature has its source in natural law philosophy, especially in the account of Thomas Aquinas. For Aquinas, an act is considered unnatural if (1) it opposes the order of right reason, or (2) it opposes the purpose or natural function of the organ. In the first sense, birth control is viewed as unnatural because it is opposed to the demands of rationally ordered activity which recognizes and requires pursuit of the goods of human nature. The good here is the good of the continuation of the species. In the second sense, birth control is unnatural because the bodily organs are used, but used in such a way that their natural function is impeded, that is, they are not directed to their proper end of human generation. Aquinas says,

> [W]herever there occurs a special kind of deformity whereby the venereal act is rendered unbecoming, there is a determinate species of lust. This may occur in two ways: First through being contrary to right reason, and that is common to all lustful vices; secondly, because in addition, it is contrary to the natural order of the venereal act as becoming to the human race; and this is called *the unnatural vice* (Aquinas, *Summa theologiae* II-II, q. 154, a. 11).

Any use of the conjugal act in such a way as to deliberately frustrate its natural power is an intrinsically evil act, an "unnatural vice." It opposes reason and opposes the proper function of the organs.

However, the encyclical moves beyond Augustine and Aquinas. It recognizes the appropriate and specific role of the exercise of the conjugal act as contributing to and cultivating the love of the spouses. It addresses the use of the conjugal act, not as excused by Augustine for the sake of procreation or for the sake of a remedy for concupiscence, but as having specific unitive and personalist ends. However, these ends are, in an evaluative sense, designated secondary and remain subordinated to the procreative end which remains primary. This use of the conjugal act must still be accomplished in such a way that violates neither the law of God nor the law of nature. In this explicit recognition of the exercise of marital rights in a situation when procreation is impossible, the encyclical says,

> Nor are those considered as acting against nature who in the married state use their right in the proper manner, although on account of natural reasons either of time or of certain defects, new life cannot be brought forth. For in matrimony as well as in the use of the matrimonial rights there are also secondary ends, such as mutual aid, the cultivating of mutual love, and the quieting of concupiscence which husband and wife are not forbidden to consider so long as they are subordinated to the primary end and so long as the intrinsic nature of the act is preserved (Pius XI 1941, 59).

Here, the practice of periodic continence receives approbation, not as a lesser evil than onanism, but as an acceptable form of conception control. Further, the good of the conjugal act in the service of the marriage and the spouses here described as, "mutual aid, the cultivating of mutual love, and the quieting of concupiscence," is explicitly recognized.

In regard to sterilization, the encyclical affirms, in the presence of a political and social climate which was marked by coercive sterilization for eugenic reasons, (1) the superiority of the right of the innocent person in regard to the exercise of the sexual faculty over the eugenic welfare of the community, (2) the superiority of the family, because more sacred, as the prior institution over the state, and (3) the superiority of the supernatural end of man over the natural end. In regard to voluntary sterilization, the encyclical affirms that the rule of an individual over the organs of the body is limited to the exercise of these in the accomplishment of their natural ends. The encyclical says,

> [P]rivate individuals have no other power over the members of their bodies than that which pertains to their natural ends; and they are not free to destroy or mutilate their members, or in any other way render themselves unfit for their natural functions, except when no other provision can be made for the good of the whole body (Pius XI 1941, 71).

Sterilization is considered a form of mutilation and is forbidden except in those instances where it serves the good of the body. This is a limited application of the principle of totality in which the good of the whole is defined in terms of the bodily good of the person.

Moral Context

In summary, the essential relevant points developed in *Casti connubii* are the following. Between the opposing poles of Gnosticism and Hedonism, *Casti connubii* frames its position on marriage describing marriage as good. While some of the essential features of marriage are disclosed, the question of the essential nature of marriage is not directly attended. The operant definition of marriage is that it is a procreative institution. Marriage is the institution in which the partners accept the role as cooperators with God in the task of procreation. The principle end of marriage is procreation. The encyclical maintains that this end was given in the institution of marriage in Paradise by God Himself in the words "Increase and multiply, and fill the earth" (ibid., 11). The complete quotation from Genesis includes the command to man to exercise rational activity, that is, of subduing or controlling the created world. It is not included in the text of the encyclical. While the notion of marriage as an intimate union appears in embryonic form in *Casti connubii*, it exercises very little controlling influence over the activities within marriage. However, the pursuit of conjugal intercourse outside of marriage is forbidden as violative of the intimate union that is marriage.

The encyclical designates as the ends of marriage the three goods of children, fidelity, and the sacrament. This delineation of the ends of marriage follows from divine revelation and from natural law principles. The end as sacrament is a graced state, the state above nature in which the sanctification of the husband and wife is accomplished in the attainment of their supernatural end. The other ends are natural ends and their specification, which may be found in revelation, follows from natural law principles.

Natural law theory as developed by the Stoics and carried by Thomas Aquinas holds two essential principles: (1) there is a natural order or rule in the universe and (2) this natural order or rule is accessible to human reason as (a) known by reason and (b) directed by reason. Aquinas says,

> [L]aw being a rule and measure, can be in a person in two ways: in one way, as in him that rules and measures; in another way, as in that which is ruled and measured, since a thing is ruled and measured, in so far as it partakes of the rule or measure. Wherefore, since all things subject to Divine providence, are ruled and measured by eternal law ... it is evident that all things partake somewhat of the eternal law, in so far as, namely, from its being imprinted on them, they derive their respective inclinations to their proper acts and ends. Now among all others, the rational creature is subject to Divine providence in the most excellent way, in so far as it partakes of a share of providence, by being provident both for itself and for others (Aquinas, *Summa theologiae* I-II, q. 91, a. 2).

In developing the natural law theory and explicitating its precepts Aquinas maintains that good is apprehended by practical reason, "good is the first thing that falls under the apprehension of practical reason" (Aquinas, *Summa theologiae* I-II, q. 94, a. 2). Aquinas further maintains that the first precept of natural law, which is based on the principle that all things seek good, is "good is to be done and pursued and evil is to be avoided" (ibid.). In the derivation of the several more specific precepts Aquinas, working from within a metaphysical context, holds that practical reason apprehends the natural inclinations or tendencies of man as good. These inclinations or tendencies are dynamic principles which press for actualization and which are ordered to the flourishing and conservation of man. Aquinas lists a methodical ordering of the natural law precepts following a methodical ordering of the inclinations identified as moving from more extensive instantiation to more specific. The first developed by Aquinas is the precept to preserve human life. It is derived from the inclination in man to live. This inclination is one which is common to man as well as to all living substances. Practical reason apprehends this inclination as good and orders the preservation of existence and the pursuit of the means of preserving human life. The second set of inclinations identified by Aquinas is the set of those which are common to man and all animals. They are the inclinations to sexual intercourse and to the education of offspring. The third set of inclinations is the set of those that are proper to humanity. Included here are the inclinations to know the truth and to live in society. In specifically addressing the goods of marriage from within this framework, but in the language of Augustine, Aquinas wrote, "offspring is the most essential good in marriage, faithfulness second and the sacrament third; even as to man it is more essential to be in nature than to be in grace, although it is more excellent to be in grace" (Aquinas, *Summa theologiae, Supplement, q. 49, a. 3).* As to the meaning of the terms essential, second, and third Aquinas wrote, "Wherefore, the first end corresponds to the marriage of man inasmuch as man is animal; the second inasmuch as man is man; the third inasmuch as man is a believer" (Aquinas, *Summa theologiae*, Supplement, q. 65, a. 1).

In operating from within the framework of this natural law position, *Casti connubii* holds that the nature of marriage has its source in the plan of God and that this plan is accessible to the reason of man as man reflects on his nature as manifest in his inclinations. In regard to the inclinations that are proper to man in the nature he has in common with other animals, man pursues sexual intercourse and pursues the education of children. The encyclical recognizes and addresses these inclinations. It identifies ends to be accomplished and specifies these ends as primary and secondary. The encyclical explicitly identifies the procreation and education of children as the primary end of marriage. In addition, the encyclical explicitly identifies as "a chief reason and purpose of marriage ... the inward formation of husband and wife" (Pius XI 1941, 24). Furthermore, the document recognizes the exercise of marital right in the pursuit of secondary ends which are identified as "mutual aid, the cultivation of mutual love, and the quieting of concupiscence" (ibid., 59). Of special significance here is the recognition of the role of sexual intercourse in the cultivation of married love even in those instances where procreation is impossible. In the designation of the ends of marriage as primary and secondary, the encyclical clearly intends a judgment of valuation. The primary end is superior to the secondary ends. If, however, the designation of the ends as primary and secondary is intended to follow the classification of Aquinas, a different evaluation is possible. For Aquinas, the primary corresponds to a lower order or more general order of existence, that is, "to the marriage of man inasmuch as man is animal," and the secondary to a higher order or more specific order of existence, that is, to the marriage of man "inasmuch as man is man."

Conjugal intercourse as the act specific to marriage is primarily a procreative act. Its exercise is appropriate within marriage in the accomplishment of reproduction. In addition, conjugal intercourse may be pursued within marriage, even when procreation is impossible, in the service of other goods of marriage, the secondary ends of "mutual aid, the cultivation of mutual love, and the quieting of concupiscence." However, the natural biology of the act of intercourse as directed to procreation must be respected. This respect for the natural act derives, in part, from the understanding that the natural function reflects eternal law and it derives, in part, from the understanding of the procreative potentiality of man as having significance beyond the individual.

Consequences for Reproductive Finality

From within the context of *Casti connubii,* a context whose ethical structure is defined by the laws of God and the natural law, all actions are forbidden which oppose the law of God and all actions are forbidden which oppose the precepts of natural law. The encyclical says,

> [A]ny use whatsoever of matrimony exercised in such a way that the act is deliberately frustrated in its natural power to generate life is an offense against the law of God and of nature, and those who indulge in such are branded with the guilt of a grave sin (ibid., 56).

Moderation of the reproductive finality within marriage must be accomplished within these proscriptions. First, in regard to the accomplishment of the reproductive finality, the encyclical, in the presence of the limited reproductive technology in its horizon, addresses, not the question of artificial insemination, but the question of intercourse outside of marriage in order to realize the good of children. The encyclical forbids the exercise of intercourse outside of marriage. The harsh words of the encyclical addressing the question of appropriateness of the possibility of the accomplishment by the male partner of the generative potentiality outside of marriage are found in the description of the rationalization in these words, "as though to suggest that the license of a base fornicating woman should enjoy the same rights as the chaste motherhood of a lawfully wedded wife" (ibid., 50).

In regard to the avoidance of the reproductive finality, the encyclical permits the practice of periodic continence. The encyclical forbids contraception understood as an act in which there is a human intervention that interferes with the accomplishment of conception. A contraceptive act is forbidden because it violates the explicit law of God as found in the Augustinian understanding of the sin of Onan or because it violates the precept of natural law. In regard to natural law violation, the determination that contraception is to be forbidden derives from the assessment of contraception as unnatural in its opposing of the natural function of the organ. There is no separate and specific determination of contraception as an act which opposes reason. Nor is there a consideration of an act which is potentially conceptive as an act which opposes reason. The question of conception or contraception as an act expressive of or violative of right reason understood as the recognition and the pursuit of a good of human nature, an objective good, in the appropriate circumstances and for the appropriate motives, is not developed within *Casti connubii*. Sterilization by medical intervention as a means of contraception is precluded in the period contemporaneous with *Casti connubii* by lack of medical/technical expertise.

Pope Pius XII: Allocutions

Introduction

Building upon the foundation of this tradition, Pope Pius XII addressed the special problems occurring in his pontificate which was marked by external and internal pressures. Among the external pressures were world war, the remarkable advances of the sciences, and rise of totalitarian governments which brought with them attacks on the physical and psychological integrity of individual persons. Among the internal pressures, in regard to marriage and its ends, were disagreements regarding the ends of marriage, the appropriate accomplishment of the ends, the hierarchy of the ends and questions regarding the very meaning of marriage. Significant among the allocutions that confronted these subjects were the Address accompanying the Sentence of the Holy Roman Rota, the Address to the Italian Medical-Biological Union of Saint Luke, the Address to the Midwives, the Address to the Association of Large Families and the Family Front, the Address to the First International Congress on the Histopathology of the Nervous System, the Address to the Twenty-Sixth Congress of the Italian Society of Urologists, the Address to the Second World Congress on Fertility and Sterility, the Address to the Seventh International Congress of Hematology, and the Address to the Tenth National Congress of the Italian Society of Plastic Surgery. Because these addresses contain statements, principles, and the application of principles that formed the parameters from within which the questions regarding the nature of marriage, the ends of marriage, and the principles that control the accomplishment of the ends of marriage were raised and from within which responses to these questions were developed, the examination of these allocutions seems appropriate. While these allocutions have not the same status as an encyclical or a conciliar document, they, as a matter of historical fact, exercised a remarkably controlling influence in doctrinal development and in the governance of human actions. The focus here will be on those texts that relate to four topics: (1) the nature and ends of marriage, (2) the avoidance of conception, (3) the accomplishment of conception, and (4) mutilation both in general and in particular as related to the mutilation of sterilization.

The Nature and Ends of Marriage

In regard to the nature of marriage and the ends of marriage, Pope Pius XII, in the early part of his pontificate, reaffirmed the essential nature of marriage as a procreative institution with emphasis on the procreative finality of marriage and on the immanent teleology of the reproductive organs beyond the individual. Pius XII continued the recognition of the two ends of marriage, that is, procreation and education as well as mutual aid and the remediation of concupiscence. Each is designated as an objective end of marriage. Each is a *finis operis*. Neither is simply an end of the agent. The procreative end is designated as primary and is valued as superior to the other ends. The specification of the nature of marriage derives from the primary end. The derivation of the nature of marriage is found in the following document of his pontificate.

> Matrimony, considered as a work and institution of nature, is a natural society, one and indivisible, specifically distinct from every other human association. It must have therefore a natural *finis operis*, one and indivisible, specifically proper and distinct from every other end. ... It follows that when several *finis operis* are assigned to the one and the same society, one of these must be prime and principal, by reason of its formal cause, in which the other ends are contained or to which others are added so that the prime cause can the more easily, surely and fully be achieved. It is necessary therefore that among the ends of matrimony there be determined the order, according to which the other *finis operis* be subordinated to the principal end, which determines the specific nature of matrimony. ... The primary and principle, one and indivisible *finis operis* of matrimony which uniquely specifies its nature is the procreation and education of the offspring (Pius XII 1944 [36], 185).

This affirmation of the essential nature of marriage, the specification of ends, and the subordination of all ends to the procreative end is subsequently reasserted in the presence of the challenge to its validity found in the claim that the procreative and personalist ends of marriage are equal. In his Address to the Midwives, Pius XII responded to the claim in these words:

> ... the appeal of certain modern writers who deny that the procreation and education of the child is the primary end of marriage, or teach that the secondary ends are not essentially subordinate to the primary end, but rather are of equal value and are independent of it, cannot be admitted (Pius XII 1951a [43], 845).

The Avoidance of Conception

In addressing the question of the avoidance of conception, Pius XII reaffirmed the nature of marriage as a procreative institution with the emphasis on the procreative finality of marriage and the immanent teleology of the reproductive organs beyond the individual to the species. In considering the nature of the act of intercourse to be a reproductive act, he regarded contraceptive measures, in keeping with the tradition of *Casti connubii*, as intrinsically evil acts and asserted that "no alleged 'indication' or need can convert an intrinsically immoral act into a moral and a lawful one" (ibid., 841). The claim that is controlling here is that for a human act to be good its object, its intention, and its circumstances must all be good. If one aspect is evil, here the object as the act of contracepting a procreative act, then the action is rendered evil. In regard to direct sterilization, he maintained that, "as a means or an end to render procreation impossible, it is a serious violation of the moral law" (ibid., 843). In addition, inasmuch as direct sterilization is an act which opposes the good of the human race, it is not included in the rights of man to the use of the parts of his body for the sake of the whole individual. Pius XII said, "We have stated in substance that direct sterilization is not authorized by man's right to dispose of his own body ... by direct sterilization we mean an act whose aim ... is to make procreation impossible" (Pius XII 1958a [50], 734). Even with these assessments of contraception and direct sterilization as opposing an end of marriage, the Pope maintained that the exercise of marital intercourse within the sterile period of the reproductive cycle was a licit method of conception control permitted to all marriages, even "throughout the entire course of the marriage" (Pius XII 1951a [43], 846), provided that there be adequate reason. The end of procreation, the end designated as the primary end, could be intentionally excluded from the marriage. Among the serious or grave reasons that might indicate the appropriateness of conception control, the Pope listed as "indications, medical, eugenic, economic and social" (ibid.). Further, he recognized that these motives might be "not rarely present" (ibid.). Following this first public approbation of periodic continence as a form of conception control, Pius XII spoke again, within a month, with approval of this method of the regulation of birth. He recognized the real difficulties encountered by the faithful in living within the married state. He said, "In our last allocution ... we affirmed the lawfulness and at the same time the limits—in truth quite broad—of a regulation of children in a manner ... compatible with the law of God" (ibid., 859). Procreation begins to be viewed within the context of the marriage rather than within the context of each and every conjugal act. In addition he expressed hope that medical science would provide a sufficiently secure foundation for the method.

The Accomplishment of Conception

In regard to the accomplishment of conception, Pius XII, in the presence of advancing reproductive technology, was called upon to address the question of artificial insemination. The objection to artificial insemination was phrased in terms of its being in violation of the personalist, relational, unitive, giving aspects of marriage. The Pope said,

> The conjugal act, in its natural structure, is a personal action, a simultaneous and immediate cooperation of the two spouses, which by the nature of the participants and the quality of the act, is the expression of the reciprocal gift, which, according to the word of the Scriptures, effects the union "in one flesh alone" (ibid., 850).

The Pope repeated similar objections to artificial insemination some five years later in terms that opposed artificial insemination as the isolation of the reproductive end of marriage from the personalist-unitive end of the spouses. He said,

> But the Church has likewise rejected the opposite attitude which would pretend to separate, in generation, the biological activity in the personal relation of the married couple. The child is the fruit of the conjugal union when that union finds full expression by bringing into play the organic functions, the associated sensible emotions, and the spirited and disinterested love which animates the union. It is in the unity of the human act that we should consider the biological

conditions of generation. Never is it permitted to separate these various aspects to the positive exclusion either of the procreative intention or of the conjugal relationship. The relationship which unites the father and the mother to their child finds its root in the organic fact and still more in the deliberate conduct of the spouses who give themselves to each other and whose will to give themselves blossoms forth and finds its true attainment in the being which they bring into the world (Pius XII 1954 [48], 470).

Several important notions regarding the marital union itself are carried in these texts. Among them is the fact that the conjugal act is regarded as having personalist and unitive, as well as procreative, significance for the spouses. The conjugal union is open to effectuation on three related levels: organic, emotional, and spiritual. The conjugal act is the reciprocal gift of the spouses, that is, in the conjugal act there occurs the self-donation of the spouses to each other. The conjugal act effectuates a union as "two become one." The union supplies the conditions for generation and nurturing of children. In addition, here there is asserted a connection between the procreative and unitive aspects in the conjugal relationship.

Mutilation in General

In addition to addressing directly the question of the avoidance of the procreative end of marital intercourse by contraception and direct sterilization and the accomplishment of conception by artificial insemination, Pius XII was called upon to examine the ethical problems of medical experimentation carried out on human subjects and of the medical treatment of human patients. Inasmuch as the principles developed in addressing these problems have application to the realization of the various ends of marriage, it seems necessary to elucidate them. In confronting these problems, he found direction in the material elements of the tradition and the structural elements of the principles of philosophy. Especially controlling from the tradition was the recognition that human life with its particular powers is a gift that humanity may use conditionally. In the face of the assaults on the bodily integrity of human beings in the immediate historical period, the Holy Father required, as prior conditions for experimentation or treatment, (1) the consent of the patient or subject, (2) adequate justification, and (3) respect for the natural powers and faculties of the patient or subject. Among the reasons proffered for the justification of the experiment or medical procedure were (a) the good of the patient, (b) the good of the community, and (c) the advancement of science. While consent and justification were seen as necessary conditions, this final condition, respect for the natural faculties of the patient or the subject, was viewed as controlling, that is, as exercising a limiting function on both consent and reason. The following statement of Pius XII summarizes the position of the tradition as constituting a framework for directing action:

> As for the patient, he is not absolute master of himself, of his body or of his soul. He cannot therefore, freely dispose of himself as he pleases. Even the reason for which he acts is of itself neither sufficient nor determining. The patient is bound to the immanent teleology laid down by nature. He has the right of use, limited by natural finality, of the faculties and powers of his human nature. Because he is a user and not a proprietor, he does not have unlimited powers to destroy or mutilate his body and its functions. Nevertheless, by virtue of the principle of totality, by virtue of his right to use the services of his organism as a whole, the patient can allow individual parts to be destroyed or mutilated when and to the extent necessary for the good of his being as a whole. He may do so to ensure his being's existence and to avoid, or, naturally, to repair serious and lasting damage which cannot otherwise be avoided or repaired (Pius XII 1952 [44], 782).

In this statement, the individual person is recognized as the steward of body and soul. In exercising stewardship, the person is permitted the use of the faculties and powers of the body and soul in accord with the immanent finality of the faculties or powers in the service of the whole. The person may not destroy the faculties or powers unless their destruction is required for the good of continued existence or that of mending or avoiding serious injury. The prominent philosophical principle operative here is the principle of totality. This principle, aided by the distinction between ordinary and extraordinary means and the principle of double effect, was to be applied to govern decisions regarding the care and treatment of patients in the presence of the technological advances of the day. The definition of the principle of totality was made explicit by Pius XII in the following:

> [T]his principle asserts that the part exists for the whole and that, consequently, the good of the part remains subordinated to the good of the whole, that the whole is a determining factor for the part and can dispose of it in its own interest. This principle flows from the essence of ideas and things and must, therefore, have an absolute value (ibid. 786).

In applying this principle to contemporaneous problems, Pius XII developed the meaning and clarified the use of the principle of totality. An important first determination is the nature of the organism to which the principle is to be applied. The initial clarification is the distinction between a physical organism and a moral organism, with the corresponding limitation of the application of the principle of totality according to the nature of the organism to which it is applied. An organism is a physical whole if it has a unity subsisting in itself. It has a unity on the level of essence. The relationship of part to whole exists, if the part as a member is an integral part of the physical unity. That is, if it

> ... is an integral part destined by all its being to be inserted in the whole organism. Outside the organism it has not, by its very nature, any sense, any finality. It is wholly absorbed by the totality of the organism to which it is attached (ibid.).

A moral organism, for example a community, is a whole which is not a physical unity subsisting in itself but a union of individuals bound together for the realization of some common action or goal. The individuals who are members of a moral whole have meaning in themselves outside that determined by their role as collaborators in the common enterprise that unites the group. The moral organism has a unity on the level of action. In regard to the community as a moral organism, it is maintained that it is "the great means intended by nature and God to regulate the exchange of mutual needs and to aid each man to develop his personality fully according to his individual and social abilities" (ibid.). From the distinction of organisms as either physical or moral wholes there follows the corresponding limitation of action in the application of the principle of totality. If the organism is a physical unit, then the extent of control over the parts is significantly different. It is said that,

> The master and user of the organism ... can dispose directly and immediately of integral parts, members and organs within the scope of their natural finality. He can also intervene, as often as and to the extent that the good of the whole demands, to paralyze, destroy, mutilate and separate the members (ibid.).

On the other hand, if the organism is a moral unit, the application of the principle is limited to the activities of the members, not the physical being of the members, in the service of the whole.

Having differentiated the various organisms as either moral or physical units, the next differentiation is the specification of the appropriate justification for the mutilating action in an organism which is a physical whole. The controlling two conditions are found in the phrases, "to the extent necessary for the good of his being as a whole" (ibid., 782) and "to the extent that the good of the whole demands" (ibid., 786). In regard to the first condition the term "good of (his being as) the whole" seems to mean not just the good of the body but the good of the person. Fr. John Connery used the phrase the "total good of the person" to signify the meaning here (Connery 1954, 602). This accords with other statements of Pius XII in which he admonished physicians to be mindful of the fact that it is persons and not bodies that are committed to their care. In addition, this accords with the recognition of the reality of the human person as a being in whom a variety of powers operates to fulfill integrated human existence. Concurrence with this assessment can be found in the evaluation of Fr. Gerald Kelly, S.J., who wrote,

> [T]o speak of the total good of the person has distinct advantages both in dealing with the medical profession and in clearly explaining certain commonly accepted solutions to modern medical problems.
> ... it is certainly easier to explain the licitness of such things as lobotomy, electro-shock therapy, and hormone treatments in terms

of the total good of the person than merely in terms of the good of
the body (Kelly 1955, 379).

In regard to the second condition, that of necessity, the meaning
seems to lie within a range that can be defined by limits that reach
from genuine utility to absolute necessity in the service of health and
life. Within these parameters, the reasons of the patient or the subject
for consenting to the mutilating procedure may vary from assurance of
existence, to repair of some actual and lasting damage, to avoidance,
in advance, of serious and lasting damage. In regard to this second
condition, Fr. Kelly wrote that the, "main point has always been that
mutilations are permissible when they are productive of a proportionate good and cannot be achieved by a less radical way" (ibid., 380).
This perception of the broadness of the range seems validated in the
affirmation by Pius XII of the many legitimate motives for plastic
surgery. Among the appropriate reasons listed were the correction,
maintenance and enhancement of physical beauty, described as, "the
perfection of attributes which already conformed to the canons of
normal aesthetics" (Pius XII 1958b [50], 959). In the service of those
reasons under the direction of the principle of totality, diseased parts
as well as healthy parts may be removed. The determination of the
appropriateness of the removal of a diseased part was governed by the
direct application of the principle of totality. If a healthy part is to be
removed, the finality of the part itself must be determined. If the part
has no finality outside the person, it may be removed. The distinction between extraordinary and ordinary means seems to govern the
application of the principle of totality here. However, if the part has
finality outside the person, as, for example, the reproductive organs,
further determinations were required.

Sterilization As Mutilation

The question of sterilization, then, as a particular form of mutilation required special treatment because the organs of reproduction
were viewed as having finality beyond the individual person, that
is, a finality directed to the good of the species. The determination
of the appropriateness of the application of the principle of totality

requires the prior determination of the sterilizing procedure as direct or indirect. The designation "direct" was applied to sterilization if the procedure intends either as an end in itself or as a means to make childbearing impossible. Pius XII said, "Direct sterilization—that is, the sterilization which aims, either as a means or as an end in itself, to render child-bearing impossible—is a grave violation of the moral law, and therefore unlawful" (Pius XII 1951b [43], 843-44). A mutilating procedure in which sterilization is an unintended or undesired consequence may be labeled indirect. In regard to this designation Fr. Kelly wrote,

> Pius XII has never, as far as I know, used the expression "indirect;" but by implication his definition of direct sterilization and by analogy his explanation of indirect killing would lead to the following description of indirect sterilization: a procedure with an accessory consequence of sterility, in no way desired or intended, though inevitably connected with necessary therapeutic treatment. In other words where sterility is merely the unintentional by-product of some needed therapeutic procedure, the sterilization is indirect (Kelly 1955, 382).

Among particular problems addressed related to the mutilation of sterilization were (1) that of removal of a diseased part of the reproductive organs, (2) that of the removal of a healthy part of the reproductive system where its continued operation might exacerbate disease related to that system, and (3) that of removal of a healthy part of the reproductive system in the presence of disease in a system of the organism unrelated to reproduction when the disease of the other system might be so exacerbated by the effect of pregnancy that the health or life of the mother would be threatened. The first is understood to be governed by the straightforward application of the principle of totality as it applies to an organ that is a part of an organism which is a physical whole. The appropriate intervention is the medical procedure, "to the extent necessary for the good of the being as a whole" (Pius XII 1952 [44], 782), directed to the removal of the diseased part. In regard to the second, Pius XII addressed directly the question of the consequence of castration on the treatment of cancer of the prostate. He said,

The decisive point is not that the amputated or paralyzed organ be itself diseased, but that its preservation or functioning directly or indirectly cause a threat to the whole body. It is quite possible that by its healthy functioning a healthy organ exerts a harmful action on a diseased organ, capable of aggravating the evil and its repercussion on the body as a whole. It can also happen that the removal of a healthy organ and the arrest of its normal function halts the evil, for example, growth in the case of cancer; or at all events essentially changes its conditions of existence. If no other means are available, surgical intervention on the healthy organ is permitted in both these cases.

... As a consequence, he who has received the use of the complete organism has the right to sacrifice a particular organ if its preservation or functioning causes a notable damage to the whole, impossible to be avoided in any other way (Pius XII 1954 [45], 673).

In the same address, Pius XII spoke to the third type of situation, that in which the removal of the Fallopian tubes or the ligation of the tubes is proposed because of the presence of disease in an organ such as the heart, lungs or kidneys which might be exacerbated by a pregnancy so that the health or life of the woman might be at risk. He said that it would be erroneous to apply the principle of totality here.

Here ... recourse is wrongly made to this principle. For in this case the danger which the mother undergoes does not come directly or indirectly from the presence or the normal functioning of the oviducts, nor from their influence upon the diseased organs, kidneys, lungs, heart. The danger is verified only if free sexual activity leads to a pregnancy which could threaten these organs already too weak or diseased. The conditions which could justify disposing the part in favor of the whole in virtue of the principle of totality are lacking (ibid., 674).

The differences in the third case from the second are several. First, the oviducts, in themselves, are not diseased. Second, the functioning of the oviducts is not systemically related to the disease of the other organs systems. And third, the understanding of the act of intercourse is one that regards it, primarily, as a reproductive act.

Consequences for the Reproductive Finality

From within the structure of the ethical principles set forth in the various addresses throughout the long pontificate of Pope Pius XII come the rules for the governance of the reproductive finality within marriage. While there is considerable continuity of the tradition from Pius XI to Pius XII, there is also development of the tradition as new issues came to the fore and as knowledge progressed. Among the advances in the understanding of the tradition are the following. Each Pontiff considered his position as developing from a natural law foundation. However in addressing the good of man, Pius XI phrased the notion in terms of the good of the body, while Pius XII spoke, repeatedly and explicitly, of the good of the whole person. The nature of the person rather than the biology of the body came to be regarded as governing. The operant definition of marriage continues to be that of a procreative institution. There are, however, occasional references to marriage as a special kind of human relationship. Nonetheless, problems of conception limitation are resolved by reference to marriage as a procreative institution rather than a conjugal union.

In regard to the avoidance of the reproductive finality, Pius XII continues the assessment of the acceptability of the practice of periodic continence. This acceptance means that the primary end of marriage can be intentionally excluded in conjugal intercourse. He recognizes a wide range of prudential reasons, "medical, eugenic, economic and social" (Pius XII 1951b [43], 846), as sufficient for the justification of the practice. This is consistent with his valuation of the appropriateness of surgical procedures for a variety of reasons defined by limits that range from genuine utility to absolute necessity in the service of health and life. Furthermore, he acknowledges the possibility that the realization of the procreative potential may be excluded throughout the course of the marriage. He continues the proscription of contraception understood as an act in which there is a direct intervention with the accomplishment of conception. Contraceptive acts are, in their objective determination, evil. They are violative of the divine positive law. They are violative of natural law precepts understood as permitting no interference with the natural function of an organ. In the presence of advancing medical/technical expertise, sterilization emerges as an effective method of direct conception control. Sterilization that directly intends contraception shares the assessment of every other contraceptive act, that is, it is intrinsically evil. And it is forbidden.

In regard to the accomplishment of conception, Pius XII continues the teaching of the tradition that the reproductive finality is to be accomplished within the marriage. There is to be no intercourse outside of marriage even to pursue the good of offspring. Furthermore, in the presence of advancing technology, he was forced to examine the question of artificial insemination. While artificial insemination intends the good of the procreative finality, the good is accomplished outside a specific act of conjugal intercourse. Artificial insemination is assessed as evil as violative of personalist, relational, unitive aspects of marriage. Here the personalist-unitive nature of marriage, not the procreative nature, controls the assessment of the proposed action. With this treatment of artificial insemination, there begins the transition in the description of the essential nature of marriage. Marriage begins to be considered a procreative union with two distinct ends, procreation and union, rather than a procreative institution.

Chapter 2

The Present:
the Recovery of the Tradition

Having completed the delineation of the tradition as framed in the documents of the immediate past, the direct examination of the documents of the tradition of the second half of the twentieth century in regard to the nature and ends of marriage follows. These documents are *Gaudium et spes, Humanae vitae,* and *Donum vitae.*

Gaudium et spes

Introduction

Gaudium et spes is a conciliar document. It was the work of the Second Vatican Council. It was approved and promulgated on December 7, 1965. It was designated a pastoral constitution because of its intention to apply the wisdom of the tradition to the contemporaneous problems. In this regard the document says, "On each of these may there shine the radiant ideals proclaimed by Christ. By these ideals may Christians be led, and all mankind be enlightened, as they search for the answers of such complexity" (*Gaudium et spes*, 46).

In the second section of the Pastoral Constitution, questions of the nature and the ends of marriage are the first addressed. The reason for this immediate attention is that the institution of marriage and the family is viewed as the pivotal institution for the person and for society. The family is the foundational community that supplies the matrix of conditions for the flourishing of the individual and that supplies, as well, the stable foundational community required for the well being of society. Several observations are made regarding problems besetting the institution of marriage. Among these problems are attacks against the nature of the institution itself. Included in the assaults against the institution are inappropriate practices within marriage and external conditions that pose threats to the survival of the marriage and the family. Included in those practices that are opposed to the very nature of marriage are polygamy, divorce, and free love. Among those that are regarded as inappropriate practices within marriage are egoism, illicit acts against the generation of children, and inordinate pursuit of pleasure. Economic, social, and psychological pressures are listed among the external threats to the institution of marriage and the family.

In response to these problems, the Fathers of the Council, specifically building on the foundation of *Casti connubii* and the addresses of Pope Pius XII, set forth the teachings of the tradition regarding the nature of marriage, a description of marital love and a recognition of its valued status, an explicitation of the several specific tasks of marriage, and directives regarding the appropriate limitation of the procreative end of marriage.

Nature and Ends of Marriage

In regard to the nature of marriage, *Gaudium et spes* says that marriage is a divine institution; it is an intimate union; and it is a sacrament. As a divine institution, marriage has a specific nature established by God. That nature is described as the constitution of an intimate union in which a relationship emerges as the "spouses mutually bestow and accept each other" (ibid., 48). This relationship is so close that it is characterized as a sacred bond, *vinculum sacrum*. Within this union various ends are to be accomplished and several benefits are to be received. These ends and goods, as enunciated in the tradition at least from Augustine to the present, are *Proles, Sacramentum, and Fides*.

As an intimate union, marriage is a particular kind of relationship, described as an "intimate partnership of married life and love" (ibid.). The union, "rooted in the conjugal covenant of irrevocable personal consent" (ibid.), comes into existence with the consent of the partners to the marriage. From this initial moment, the union itself develops as "a man and a woman, by their compact of conjugal love 'are no longer two, but one flesh' (Matt. 19:6)" (ibid.). The initial experience of two in one flesh in the exercise of the conjugal act is an immediate experience of the oneness, as each gives and accepts each other in "a mutual gift of two persons" (ibid.). However, the actualization of the complete unity, the relationship itself, that "intimate unity of persons and actions" (ibid.) is accomplished only in time. The nature of marriage as an intimate union between persons is further emphasized when *Gaudium et spes* asserts, as did *Casti connubii* before it, that marriage persists even when there are no children. The document says,

> Marriage to be sure is not intended solely for procreation; rather, its very nature as an unbreakable compact between persons, and the welfare of children, both demand that the mutual love of the spouses be embodied in a rightly ordered manner, that it grow and ripen. Therefore marriage persists as a whole manner and communion of life, and maintains its value and indissolubility, even when, despite the often intense desire of the couple, offspring are lacking (ibid., 50).

The importance of marital intercourse to the sustenance and the cultivation of the marriage union is explicitly recognized in *Gaudium et spes*. Because the marital union supplies the matrix of conditions both for the nurturing of already existing children and for the possibility of additional children, the continuation of the union itself is essential. The document says,

> [W]here the intimacy of married life is broken off, its faithfulness can sometimes be imperiled and its quality of fruitfulness ruined, for then the upbringing of the children and the courage to accept new ones are both endangered (ibid., 51).

As sacramental, marriage is a graced state. Its sacramental status is the gift of Christ in His presence and in His example, that is, the loving and faithful relationship of Christ to the Church which serves as the exemplar relationship for the marriage relationship. The effects of the sacrament are several, including the strengthening of the union, the sanctification of the partners, and the proper direction of the children. In regard to the firmness of the marital union, the grace of the sacrament affects the union in such a way as to render it indissoluble. The document says in regard to the presence of Christ in this union that, "He abides with them thereafter so that just as He loved the Church and handed himself over on her behalf, the spouses may love each other with perpetual fidelity through mutual self-bestowal" (ibid., 48). The formation of the union, by love and in love, supplies the matrix of conditions in which the two ends of procreation and education of children and of the perfection of the partners are to be accomplished. In addition to fortifying the union, the grace of the sacrament also aids the accomplishment of the transcendental end of the partners in the marriage. The document says,

> By virtue of this sacrament, as spouses fulfill their conjugal and family obligations, they are penetrated with the spirit of Christ, which suffuses their whole lives with faith, hope and charity. Thus they increasingly advance the perfection of their own personalities, as well as their mutual sanctification, and hence contribute jointly to the glory of God (ibid.).

Within this union, the grace of the sacrament is efficacious in the fulfillment of the natural perfections of each partner, as well as in the elevation of each to holiness. In addition, the grace of the sacrament is efficacious in the task of parenting. It exercises a transforming effect on the married love of the parents to "aid and strengthen them in the sublime office of being father and mother" (ibid.).

Description and Assessment of Marital Love

The description of marital love and the recognition of its valued status follows with a reminder of the scriptural recognition of the role of conjugal love and affection in developing and nourishing the marriage. Here, marital love is explicitly recognized as good. In the texts cited, many of the constitutive elements of the marital union are brought into focus. Among them are the formation of the marital union, the oneness that results "as two become one flesh," as found in the Genesis texts 2:18 and 22-24. The joy of the marriage, as well as the enhancement of the marriage and the enhancement of the status of the husband by the presence and industry of the good wife, is noted from Proverbs 5:18-20 and 31:10-31. The help and support of the husband and wife, over a lifetime, is found in the text of Tobit 8:4-8. The sexual attractiveness of the spouses to each other is celebrated throughout the Song of Songs. The gift of each to the other is found among the topics in 1 Corinthians 7:3-6. The model of the love of Christ for the church as the exemplar for married love, the dedication in marriage such that the beauty of the spouse, "pure and faultless, without spot or wrinkle or any other imperfection," is accomplished, and the union of the marriage are found in Ephesians 5:25-33.

Marital love is described as fully human. It is the love of two persons of each other. The document says that,

> [I]t is directed from one person to another through an affection of the will; it involves the good of the whole person, and therefore can enrich the expression of the body and the mind with a unique dignity, ennobling these expressions as special ingredients and signs of the friendship distinctive of marriage (ibid., 49).

Marital love, as sacramental, is transformed by God who, "has judged [it] worthy of special gifts, healing, perfecting and exalting gifts of grace and charity" (ibid.). Marital love, as marked by its own specific natural and graced characteristics makes possible the gift of the spouses to each other and the reception of the spouses by each other. This gift is described as, "that mutual self-giving by which spouses enrich each other with a joyful and a ready will" (ibid.).

Procreative End of Marriage

In the specification of the tasks of marriage, *Gaudium et spes* reaffirms the natural ordination of marriage and intercourse to the procreation and nurturing of children. This natural ordination follows from the nature of the institution as a heterosexual, procreative union in its creation by God. The document specifically refers to the reason for the union in the words of the biblical passage from Genesis in which God said, "it is not good for man to be alone" (Gen 2:18). The heterosexual nature of the marital institution is also attributed directly to the intention of God, "Who made man from the beginning male and female" (Matt 19:4). Among the reasons for the creation of humanity as male and female, is that the union, as procreative, may participate in the divine work of creation in fulfilling the Genesis command: "Increase and multiply" (Gen 1:28). In focusing on this specific procreative function of marriage, the document clearly recognizes the role of conjugal love in the disposition of the partners to enable their cooperation with the creative and redeeming love of God in their vocation as parents.

When the document addresses the good of children, it asserts that goodness in two senses, that is, the different but related ends of the existence itself of children and the end of the nurturing of children. In regard to their existence, inasmuch as marriage is, specifically a procreative institution, the existence of children brings about the realization of that end; hence, they "are really the supreme gift of marriage" (ibid., 50). As a consequence of the existence of children, there results an ontological transformation as the partners of the marital union become parents. As parents, the partners have specific functions to fulfill in regard to their children. In the nurturing of children, which is the accomplishment of the proper education of children, the end of parenting is accomplished. The obligations of parents to procreate and to educate are to be fulfilled reasonably, responsibly, and generously. The document says,

> [T]hey will fulfill their task with human and Christian responsibility, and, with docile reverence toward God, will make decisions by common counsel and effort. Let them thoughtfully take into account both their own welfare and that of their children, those already born and those which the future may bring. Let them thoughtfully take into account both the material and spiritual conditions of the times as well as of their state in life. Finally they should consult the interests of the family group, of temporal society, and of the Church herself. The parents themselves should ultimately make this judgment in the sight of God. ... they cannot proceed arbitrarily, but must always be governed according to a conscience dutifully conformed to the divine law itself, and should be submissive toward the Church's teaching office, which authentically interprets that law in the light of the Gospel. That divine law reveals and protects

the integral meaning of conjugal love, and impels it toward a truly human fulfillment (ibid.).

Because the procreative end is to be exercised reasonably and responsibly as well as generously, the document recognizes that the present circumstances of a particular marriage may be such that the transmission of new life is not appropriate. The limitation of conception, reasonably and responsibly, is a good. It is not contrary to the institutional character of marriage. *Gaudium et spes* recognizes, at the same time, the importance of the exercise of the conjugal act to the life and vitality of the conjugal union. And, it recognizes the necessity of the marital union as providing the appropriate set of conditions for the nurturing of children. The accomplishment and maintenance of all these goods is realistically recognized as not unproblematic. However, in seeking a solution to the problem of the goods to be accomplished, the ends must be accomplished in accord with divine law which governs both the transmission of life and the realization of conjugal love. Here, *Gaudium et spes* appears to be developing an aspect of the natural law tradition that is absent from prior documents of the tradition in their treatment of the regulation of the procreative end. That aspect is the consideration of an act inasmuch as it opposes, not the natural function of an organ, but as it opposes reason. An act which is potentially conceptive, that is, good in its objective determination, may be assessed as morally evil because either the appropriate circumstance or the appropriate motive is lacking. The precepts of natural law command action under the rule of reason. In the exercise of reason, humanity shares in a special way in eternal law, that is, "by being provident both for itself and for others" (Aquinas, *Summa theologiae* I-II, q. 91, a. 2). The document calls attention to the fact that there can exist no contradiction "between the divine laws pertaining to the transmission of life and those pertaining to authentic conjugal love" (*Gaudium et spes*, 51).

In addition, the document reaffirms the traditional view that the control of humanity over human life is limited to stewardship. As a consequence, abortion and infanticide are immediately eliminated as possible means for the limitation of offspring. Considered as the direct taking of innocent human life, they are dismissed as "unspeakable crimes" (ibid.). Conception control, which may be characterized as good in intention and good in particular circumstances, suffers the loss of its integral goodness, if the action in itself is not good. In this regard the document says,

> Hence when there is a question of harmonizing conjugal love with the responsible transmission of life, the moral aspect of any procedure does not depend solely on sincere intentions or on an evaluation of motives, but must be determined by objective standards. These, based on the nature of the human person and his acts preserve the full sense of mutual self-giving and human procreation in the context of true love (ibid.).

The objective standards which govern the moral determination of the action are said to have their foundation, not in the intrinsic finality of an isolated bodily organ, but in the nature of the human person. And, here, the human person that is to serve as the foundation is the person who is determined in a particular way, that is, as having consented to marriage. It follows, then, that the objective determination of any conjugal act depends on its fulfillment of the ends of marriage. And the ends of marriage are specifications of the essence of marriage. This conclusion is made explicit in the document in the requirement that the act, "preserve the full sense of mutual self-giving and human procreation in the context of true love" (ibid.).

Limitation of Reproductive Finality

In considering the question of the appropriate means of conception control, *Gaudium et spes* cites particular elements in the tradition, refers to particular documents as sources of the correct teaching in regard to conception control, and reserves the resolution of certain specific questions for future examination. The elements of the tradition include the natural law foundation of the teaching and the claim that certain acts are intrinsically evil. The natural law foundation of the teaching is not here the claim that biological laws are determining, but rather that the essence or nature of the person, a rational being, is the determinant. The latter claim, regarding the intrinsic evil of certain actions, dates back at least to Saint Paul who said, "Evil may not be done in order that good may come from it" (Romans 3:8). The specification of the moral goodness of an action as requiring that it be good in intention, circumstances, and object continues through the long history of the tradition. It is explicitly developed by Thomas Aquinas in the *Summa theologiae I-II* in Question 18 which treats of the specification of human action as good or evil. There Aquinas says,

> Nothing hinders an action that is good in one of the ways men-
> tioned above, from lacking goodness in another way. And thus it
> may happen that an action which is good in its species or in its
> circumstances, is ordained to an evil, or vice versa. However, an
> action is not good simply, unless it is good in all those ways: since
> "evil results from any single defect, but good from the complete
> cause," as Dionysius says (*DIV. NOM. IV*) (Aquinas, *Summa theo-
> logiae* I-II, q. 18, a. 4, ad 3).

Among the contemporary defenders of the requirement of integral goodness of the human action in the form *bonum ex integra causa et malum ex quocumque defectu* are John Finnis, Germain Grisez, Ronald Lawler, William May, and Joseph Boyle.

The documents, specifically cited in *Gaudium et spes,* include *Casti connubii* of Pius XI and certain allocutions of Pius XII. These documents contain prohibitions of contraception for inappropriate reasons, such as selfishness and pursuit of pleasure, and also prohibitions of contraception for appropriate reasons when the contraceptive acts, in their objective determination, are intrinsically evil, that is, those which violate the law of God and/or the law of nature. Under specific direction, the resolution of more concrete questions was held in abeyance for study by a special commission.

Among the significant teachings of *Gaudium et spes* as developments within the tradition the following are included: (1) the essential nature of marriage, (2) the specific ends of marriage, (3) the role of conjugal intercourse, (4) responsible parenthood, and (5) respect for the tradition. In regard to the first, the claim that marriage has an essential nature persists. However, there is explicit emphasis on the essence of marriage as an intimate partnership of marital life and love, rather than the consideration of marriage, exclusively, as a procreative institution. Marriage is described as a covenant between two persons in which there is a mutual giving and accepting of persons. The human person, not the body, is offered and received. The claim that the union that is marriage persists even when there are no children echoes the similar claim of *Casti connubii* and is consistent with other teachings in the tradition. In regard to the second, union and procreation continue to be acknowledged as the ends of marriage. However, the ends and purposes of marriage are no longer designated as primary or secondary. There appears no hierarchical structure of values and no subordination of ends and purposes. In regard to the third, conjugal intercourse as an expression of marital love is valued in itself. Conjugal intercourse does not need a special motive beyond that of marital love, such as procreation or remediation of concupiscence, to give it moral character. In addition there is an explicit recognition of the role of conjugal intercourse in the nurturing of the marital union. Fidelity and indissolubility appear as requirements and characteristics of the marriage considered as an intimate union in which the perfection of the partners is to be realized, rather than as a requirement of marriage as a procreative union. Understood in this latter sense, marriage would seem to require only a relative indissolubility, lasting as long as the children remain children, that is, are dependent. In regard to the fourth, the opportunity to procreate, which emphasizes human creative power, is characterized as an act in collaboration with God. Procreation and education are acts marked by special dignity. In procreation and education, the parents are carriers and imitators of the love of God. However, this opportunity carries with it the obligation that it be exercised consciously, responsibly, and generously. The decision regarding the number of children is, ultimately, the prudential judgment of the parents. Finally, the teachings of the tradition exercise a limiting function on the manner of exercising control of the number of children.

Pontifical Commission Report

To aid in the resolution of the more specific questions deliberately left unanswered at the conclusion of the Second Vatican Council, Pope Paul VI turned to the Pontifical Commission for the Study of the Problems of Population, Family and Births that had been established by Pope John XXIII in March of 1963. Paul VI enlarged the Commission and charged it with the task of gathering knowledge regarding married life and the regulation of conception within marriage. The Commission completed its work and forwarded its findings to the Holy Father. The Majority Report that issued from the members of the Commission included the assessment that the actualization of the procreative potentiality be understood as a requirement of the entire course of the marriage rather than a requirement of every single act of intercourse within the marriage. The Report argued that the moral specification of marriage, considered as an act in itself, derives not from particular acts which constitute partial aspects of the marriage but from the set of acts throughout the duration of the marriage. Following the reception of the findings of the Study Commission, Pius VI issued the encyclical *Humanae vitae.*

Pope Paul VI: *Humanae vitae*

Introduction

The focus of *Humanae vitae* is on the transmission of human life within marriage. While the encyclical characterizes the transmission of human life as a serious duty for the marriage partners, it also recognizes marriage as a joyous act in which the marriage partners participate in the creative activity of God. The encyclical also notes that the responsible exercise of the procreative powers of the parents is sometimes accompanied by rather considerable difficulties. In addressing the serious privilege of the regulation of conception in the presence of these difficulties, the encyclical first examines the cultural background from within which the questions and challenges are framed. The encyclical, then, makes explicit the doctrinal principles which supply the elements of the tradition that are to be appropriated for the fashioning of the response. It, then, responds to specific methods of birth regulation. The encyclical concludes with a set of pastoral directives.

Among the various elements that constituted the socio-cultural background in which the encyclical was issued were global, familial, and individual problems, the progress of the sciences as they impact on human life, and the occurrence of the transformation of several values related to the understanding of marriage and its ends. The encyclical notes that on a global level, population, especially in the newly emerging countries, is increasing more rapidly than the resources requisite for sustaining that population. The encyclical recognizes that economic problems can wreak havoc within the family in the task of supporting and educating their children. In addition, *Humanae vitae* adverts to several value changes. The first of the value transformations has its source in the fact of the changed role of women and, as a consequence, of the changing perception of women in the contemporaneous society. The second value change derives from the development of the understanding of the role of marital love, as expressed in the conjugal act, to the marriage union. Finally, the encyclical takes note of the progression of the sciences in affording humankind increasing direction over the forces of nature in the service of humanity.

In the presence of these pressures and advances, the encyclical affirms the competence of the Church as teacher and as interpreter of the tradition as the tradition carries meaning for the problems regarding the nature of marriage, the exercise of the marital act, and the regulation of conception and birth within marriage. The encyclical cites natural law, revelation, and the teaching authority of the Church as the sources of the principles of its moral reasoning on marriage. That authority was conferred by Christ on the Apostles and it continues to the present. The document says that the teaching is "founded on the natural law, illuminated and enriched by divine revelation" (Paul VI 1968, 4). The document expands on the multifaceted source of the teaching in the following:

> It is in fact indisputable, as our predecessors have on numerous occasions declared, that Jesus Christ, when communicating to Peter and the Apostles his divine authority and sending them to teach

his commandments to all nations constituted them guardians and authentic interpreters of the whole moral law, that is to say, not only of the law of the Gospel, but also of the natural law. For the natural law, too, is an expression of the will of God, and it likewise must be observed faithfully to attain salvation (ibid.).

In concluding the sketch of the background from which the encyclical emerged, the document acknowledges the contributions of those with special skills and experience in the pursuit of resolution of the difficult questions posed for the Church at this time. These contributions include those offered by the members of the Special Pontifical Commission in its majority and minority reports. The grateful reception of these reports is attenuated by the assessment of the encyclical that the criteria applied in the resolution of the questions of birth regulation were at variance with the continuous teaching of the tradition and the assessment that the ultimate resolution remained a papal prerogative.

Marriage: Nature and Ends

The explicitation in *Humanae vitae* of the doctrinal principles and the application of those principles to the practices within marriage begins with a description of human life which recognizes in it multiple personal dimensions, with its natural and supernatural goals, and its flourishing in the accomplishment of integrated human living. It continues with a definition of marriage, a phenomenological description of the elements that constitute conjugal love, and a consideration of the multiple obligations that mark responsible parenthood. The document, then, addresses, from within the context of the principles and ideals which are operative and formative in marriage, the critical issue of the appropriate means of birth regulation. The section on doctrinal principles draws to closure with a listing of the serious possible consequences of the use of inappropriate methods of birth regulation and a reaffirmation of the role of the Church as the carrier of moral law.

Within the text of *Humanae vitae* the following definition of marriage is offered:

> Marriage is ... a wise institution of the Creator to realize in mankind his design of love. By means of the reciprocal personal gift which is proper and exclusive to them, husband and wife tend toward that communion of their being whereby they help each other toward personal perfection in order to collaborate with God in the begetting and rearing of new lives. For baptized persons, moreover, marriage takes on the dignity of a sacramental sign of grace, inasmuch as it represents the union of Christ and the Church (ibid., 8).

This specification of the reality of marriage includes many elements of the tradition. Among them are its divine institution and its sacramental character. The reciprocal personal giving and receiving that is appropriate and specific to marriage echoes the mutual bestowal and acceptance of each other that found expression in *Gaudium et spes*. Similarly, the intimate union of *Gaudium et spes* is reaffirmed here as the communion of the very personal being of the spouses. The reality, the union which aspires to instantiate in its living the union of Christ and the Church, that results from the communion of being is to supply the matrix of conditions essential for the perfection of the husband and wife. The union is, at the same time, to supply the matrix of conditions in which a specific perfection is to be accomplished. That perfection is that of the actualization of the capacities of the spouses to exercise the serious responsibility of the procreation and nurturing of children.

Description of Marital Love

The document has a description of married love and a delineation of some of the essential characteristics of conjugal love. The nobility of married love is affirmed and its source is indicated in, "God, who is Love, (1 Jn. 4:8) 'the Father, from whom all fatherhood in heaven and on earth receives its name' (Eph. 3:15)" (ibid.). Among the characteristics that are required of married love are its humanness, its plenitude, its faithfulness and exclusivity, and its fruitfulness. As human, married love is expressive of all the qualities that mark human existence. It is both sensitive and spiritual. It is an affective tending that is responsive to the conative will. Conjugal love disposes to the formation of the marital union, described in the encyclical as, "a way that, husband and wife become one heart and one soul" (ibid., 9). While conjugal love enriches the union with its joys, it also fortifies the union making it an enclosure from within which it is possible for the partners to realize their human perfection and to withstand the sorrows and vicissitudes of this life.

As full, married love is expressive of a particular kind of human friendship, in which there is the magnificent sharing of all things by the spouses. This magnificent sharing is characterized as *magno animo* (ibid.). When the marital love is true love, the spouses give as freely to each other as they receive from each other. Marriage is distinguished by a love that is faithful and exclusive until the end of life. While faithfulness and exclusivity are promised at the beginning of marriage with the acceptance of the bond, and while manifested in physical faithfulness and exclusivity from the beginning of the marriage, they become an accomplished personal reality only in the becoming of the marriage. *Humanae vitae* recognizes both the difficulty of fidelity as well as the enhancement of the marriage by faithfulness. The encyclical says of this fidelity,

> A fidelity, that can at times be difficult, but which is always possible, always noble and meritorious, as no one can deny. The example of so many married persons down through the centuries shows not only that fidelity is according to the nature of marriage but also that it is the source of profound and lasting happiness (ibid.).

The fruitfulness that characterizes marital love displays its fecundity in two ways. One is in the generation of the union, "the communion between husband and wife" (ibid.). The other is in the procreation and nurturing of children. In regard to the latter, the encyclical reasserts the claim of *Gaudium et spes* which says, "Matrimony and conjugal love are ordained by their very nature to the procreation and education of children. Children are the most precious gift of marriage and confer upon their parents the greatest good" (ibid.).

Procreative Responsibility in Marriage

The marvelous privilege of parenthood requires that the spouses understand and attend seriously to the multiple obligations in actualizing that privilege. Among the concerns cited in the encyclical that require the attention of the spouses are respect for the biological processes, concern for the physical, economic, social, and psychological conditions, and regard for the objective moral order. All of these interrelated and valid concerns, which are designated duties, must be respected by the marriage partners. Respect for the biological processes requires that both reason and nature be accorded their appropriate roles in actualizing these natural processes. Nature, here the biological processes, has a limiting function to exercise on reason. And, at the same time, reason has a commanding influence over nature. The encyclical says,

> In relation to the biological processes, responsible parenthood means knowing and respecting the functions of these processes; the intellect discovers in the power of giving life biological laws that are part of the human person. In relation to the tendencies of instinct and of the passions, responsible parenthood means the necessary mastery that reason and will must exercise over them (ibid., 10).

Here, the encyclical cites as the source for its position on the role accorded both nature and reason, the natural law teaching as found in the work of Thomas Aquinas. The locus of the natural law teaching of Aquinas is the *"De legibus* Treatise*"* of the *Summa theologiae.* The specific text cited, as was the case with other documents of the tradition, is Question 94, article 2 which deals with the derivation of the several principles of natural law. In deriving the various principles of natural law, Aquinas examines the natural inclinations of the human being as operations which manifest the nature of a living human substance. These inclinations press for actualization and in their actualization are perfective of the human person. The natural inclinations, themselves, are given. They are constituent parts of the nature of the human person. Aquinas says of these inclinations that they, "are naturally apprehended by reason as being good, and consequently as objects of pursuit, and their contraries as evil, and objects of avoidance" (Aquinas, *Summa theologiae* I-II, q. 92, a. 2). The natural inclinations that Aquinas examines that are especially relevant here are the inclinations that humanity has in common with all animals. Of those inclinations, Aquinas specifies two, the inclination to sexual intercourse and the inclination to nurture offspring. Both of these inclinations are naturally apprehended by reason as good and the actualization of each contributes to the flourishing of integral humanism. However, their actualization, as is the case with the actualization of all natural inclinations, must be accomplished under the one rule of reason, which is "good is to be done and pursued, and evil is to be avoided" (Aquinas, *Summa theologiae* I-II, q. 94, a. 2). Aquinas says,

> All the inclinations of any parts whatsoever of human nature, e.g., of the concupiscible and irascible parts, in so far as they are ruled by reason, belong to the natural law, and are reduced to the one first precept, as stated above: so that the precepts of the natural law are many in themselves, but are based on one common foundation (ibid., ad 2).

In this second article of Question 94 on Natural Law, Aquinas is simply listing several of the precepts of the law following an ordering from more general to more specific, that is, from inclinations that humanity has in common with all living substances to inclinations that are specific to the human person. He does not directly take up the question as to which inclination takes precedence in a conflict situation or the question of the circumstances in which the suppression of a natural inclination, whether for a determinate or an indeterminate time, is appropriate. However, in the fourth article of the same question, Aquinas specifically recognizes that the domain of practical reason is that of the contingent affairs of human action rather than the necessary conclusions of speculative reason. Because this is the case, the actualization of a natural inclination, apprehended in general as good, might be deemed inappropriate in a specific situation. In elucidating the question at hand he gives, as an example, the case in which goods belonging to one person are held in trust by another. He says,

But as to the proper conclusions of the practical reason, neither is the truth or the rectitude the same for all, nor where it is the same, is it equally known by all. Thus it is right and true for all to act according to reason: and from this principle it follows as a proper conclusion, that goods entrusted to another should be restored to their owner. Now this is true for the majority of cases: but it may happen in a particular case that it would be injurious, and therefore unreasonable, to restore goods held in trust; for instance if they are claimed for the purpose of fighting against one's country. And this principle will be found to fail the more, according as we descend further into detail, e.g., if one were to say that goods held in trust should be restored with such and such a guarantee, or in such and such a way; because the greater the number of conditions added, the greater the number of ways in which the principle may fail, so that it might be not right to restore or not to restore (Aquinas, *Summa theologiae* I-II, q. 94, a. 4).

Humanae vitae, in applying these principles developed by Aquinas, recognizes the good that is the fulfillment of the natural inclination to nurture children. However, the encyclical calls attention to the fact that responsible parenthood requires that those who would exercise that privilege be attentive to the conditions in which they would actualize their prerogative. Particular circumstances including economic, psychological, physical, and social conditions must be considered. And, here, prudential reason must exercise its controlling power. If the circumstances which define the parameters from within which the procreative powers would be exercised are inappropriate, then the objectively good action, the fulfillment of the natural inclination to procreate, would be rendered evil by that circumstance, and, hence, it must be avoided. This assessment of the determining power of circumstances is consonant with the evaluation of human acts in the moral philosophy of Aquinas. In his account of human acts, Aquinas compares the nature of human acts with the nature of natural substances and he evaluates the isomorphism of the circumstances of human actions and the accidents of natural substances. He says,

> In natural things, it is to be noted that the whole fulness of perfection due to a thing, is not from the mere substantial form, that gives it its species; since a thing derives much from supervening accidents, as man does from shape, color, and the like; and if any one of these accidents be out of due proportion, evil is the result. So it is with action. For the plenitude of its goodness does not consist wholly in its species, but also in certain additions which accrue to it by reason of certain accidents; and such are its due circumstances. Wherefore if something be wanting that is requisite as a due circumstance the action will be evil (Aquinas, *Summa theologiae* I-II, q. 18, a. 3).

The application of these notions developed by Aquinas to the question of conception regulation in *Humanae vitae* would seem to require the conclusion that the accomplishment of the reproductive finality in inappropriate circumstances is an evil action. This line of reasoning is not explicitly developed in the encyclical, which focuses primarily on the objective determination of the act.

In addition to respect for the biological processes and attendance to the circumstances surrounding the exercise of the procreative potentiality, the encyclical reminds the marriage partners of their obligation to act according to an objectively determined moral order. Knowledge of this moral order, which has its source in eternal law, is the accomplishment of a rightly formed conscience. The notion of rightly formed conscience carries with it the requirements of sufficient knowledge and correct moral development. The encyclical says,

> Responsible parenthood also and above all implies a more profound relationship to the objective moral order established by God, and of which right conscience is the faithful interpreter. The responsible exercise of parenthood implies, therefore, that husband and wife recognize fully their duties toward God, toward themselves, toward the family and toward society, in a correct hierarchy of values. ... they must conform their actions to the creative intention of God, expressed in the very nature of marriage and of its acts, and manifested by the constant teaching of the Church (Paul VI 1968, 10).

Doctrinal Principles

Having completed the characterization of conjugal love, the consideration of the multiple obligations that distinguish responsible parenthood, and the assertion of the existence of an objective moral order, the encyclical makes explicit the doctrinal principles that are derived from the prior considerations and that are to direct the critical issue of birth regulation. These principles have their foundation in natural law. That is, they are, "a teaching founded on natural law, illumined and enriched by divine Revelation" (ibid.). They include the following. First, the marriage act is an act which is procreative and unitive. Second, the procreative end and unitive end are inseparable. In regard to the first, the marriage act tends toward the transmission of human life and it tends toward the enhancement and fortification of the marital union. The encyclical recognizes both these natural inclinations that press for actualization in the marital act in the following:

> Indeed, by its intimate structure, the conjugal act, while closely uniting husband and wife, makes them apt for the generation of new lives, according to laws inscribed in the very being of man and woman. By safeguarding both these essential aspects, the unitive and the procreative, the conjugal act preserves in its fullness the sense of true mutual love and its ordination to man's most high vocation to parenthood. We think that men of our day are particularly capable of confirming the deeply reasonable and human character of this fundamental principle (ibid., 12).

Following the specification of the two essential aspects of the marital act, *Humanae vitae* sets forth the second claim. In regard to that claim, the encyclical maintains that there is an indissoluble connection between the unitive signification and the procreative signification of the conjugal act. The existence of this indissoluble connection, which is said to have its foundation in divine law, and in natural law as the participation in divine law, is asserted to be a recurrent teaching of the church. However, there is no evidence offered in the text for the natural law foundation, understood as the apprehension by practical reason of the inseparable connection of the procreative and unitive aspects of conjugal intercourse, of the inseparability principle. In addition, there is no disclosure of enrichment or illumination by a special divine revelation. There is, moreover, no direct citation in the text of the encyclical as to the antecedents of this teaching in the tradition. However, in the immediate past, the notion of inseparable connection begins to appear in the later allocutions of Pope Pius XII, especially in those in which he addresses the question of artificial insemination. There, he was addressing the accomplishment of the reproductive finality in a manner that isolates the reproductive end of marriage from the personalist-unitive end of marriage. He said, "Never is it permitted to separate these various aspects to the positive exclusion either of the procreative intention or of the conjugal relationship" (Pius XII 1956 [48], 470). No such similar claim was made by Pius XII in the earlier allocutions, which address the question of conception limitation within marriage, for the necessity of the actualization of the personalist-unitive aspects of the conjugal act.

Humanae vitae maintains that so binding is this connection that its deliberate sundering is forbidden. The encyclical, in ascribing a connection that is characterized as indissoluble between the meaning of the unitive and procreative inclinations, says, "the inseparable connection, willed by God and which man may not break on his own initiative" (Paul VI 1968, 12). It would seem, then, that every conjugal act must be expressive of both meanings at least in the very minimal fashion that there be no direct or human intervention or interference in the actualization of either. That is, there may be no deliberate dissociation of the meaning of these distinct and determinate potentialities in the exercise of the conjugal act. In directing attention, specifically, to the procreative power the encyclical says, "any use of matrimony whatsoever must remain in itself destined to the procreation of human life" (ibid., 11). While there may be no deliberate separation of the meanings, the document does recognize that the procreative potentiality, as a matter of biological fact, is not actualized and cannot be actualized in every act of marital intercourse. The reproductive and unitive potentialities are separable. The biphasic cycle of the woman precludes the possibility of conception in every act of marital intercourse. This cycle of fertility/infertility is viewed as natural. *Humanae vitae* claims that this biphasic cycle is part of the design of the Creator and is assessed as having as its purpose the appropriate spacing of conception. In respect to the natural infertility of such acts of conjugal intercourse the encyclical maintains these acts "do not cease to be legitimate if, for causes independent of the will of husband and wife, they are foreseen to be infertile, because they remain ordained to expressing and strengthening their union" (ibid.). This is consistent with the claim of the earlier documents of the tradition, especially those of Pius XI and Pius XII, that accept the practice of periodic continence as a method of conception regulation. The controlling limitation is that nothing may interfere with the natural act. And the natural act is understood here in its physical/procreative sense.

Consequences of Inseparability Principle

The encyclical maintains that to actualize conjugal life from within the parameters defined by the doctrinal principles of *Humanae vitae* is to act in a manner consonant with the design of God and in a manner to bring about the flourishing of the marriage. The consequences of the application of the doctrinal principle of the indissoluble connection between the significance of the procreative potentiality and the significance of the unitive potentiality are several. The first attended to by the encyclical regards the unitive aspect. It requires that every conjugal act be expressive of the love of the spouses for each other. The document says,

> It is in fact justly observed that a conjugal act imposed upon one's partner without regard for his or her conditions and legitimate desires is not a true act of love, and therefore denies a requirement of the moral right order in the relations between husband and wife (ibid., 13).

The encyclical then addresses the procreative aspect within an act expressive of conjugal love. *Humanae vitae* maintains that to actualize the unitive meaning in conjugal love and to suppress the reproductive potentiality is to act in a manner opposed to the inherent structure of marriage. The encyclical says,

Hence, one who reflects carefully must also recognize that an act of mutual love that prejudices the capacity to transmit life that God the Creator, according to particular laws, inserted therein, is in contradiction with the design constitutive of marriage and the will of the Author of life. Those who make use of the divine gift while destroying, even if only partially, its significance and its finality, act contrary to the nature of both man and woman and of their most intimate relationship, and therefore contradict also the plan of God and his will. On the other hand, those who enjoy the gift of conjugal love while respecting the laws of the generative process show that they acknowledge themselves to be not the masters of the sources of human life, but rather the ministers of the design established by the Creator. In fact just as man does not have unlimited dominion over the body in general, so also, with particular reason, he has no such dominion over his generative faculties as such, because of their intrinsic ordination to the bringing into being of life, of which God is the principle. "Human life is sacred," John XXIII recalled; "from its very inception it directly involves the creative action of God" (ibid., 13).

This text appears to be the source of the apothegm of the contemporary birth control debate, "No intercourse without reproduction; no reproduction without intercourse" (Connery 1982).

Along with the indissoluble connection between the unitive significance and the reproductive significance, several important themes recurrent in the tradition and important relative to conception regulation are repeated in this text. Among them are (1) the natural law foundation, (2) the human role of stewardship of creation, and (3) the assessment of human life as sacred. In regard to the assertion that the position follows from natural law, there is a single source of the theory and there are several related notions of the theory. The natural law notions operative in *Humanae vitae* are representative of the thought of Thomas Aquinas. While the encyclical inclines to the will aspect of the activity of the Creator in the description of the origin of the design of the created world, the emphasis of Aquinas in developing the theory and in relating it to eternal law inclines more to the reason than to the will. In this regard Aquinas says,

> But in order that the volition of what is commanded may have the nature of law, it needs to be in accord with some rule of reason. And in this sense is to be understood the saying that the will of the sovereign has the force of law; otherwise the sovereign's will would savor of lawlessness rather than of law (Aquinas, *Summa theologiae* I-II, q. 90, a. 1, ad 3).

This reflects, in general, the intellectualist orientation operative in the work of Aquinas. Of the related notions, the first is that natural law is accessible to human reason. In this regard, the encyclical remarks that contemporary humanity, not just those operating from within a particular faith context, is capable of according rational consent to these notions (Paul VI 1968, 12) and again, that from the consideration of the act of mutual love it should be possible to conclude that interference with the transmission of life constitutes a violation of conjugal love (ibid.). The second of the related notions is that the created world is made of beings that are essentially determined, that is, beings which have specific natures. Humanity has a nature; man has a nature; marriage has a nature; and the generative faculties have a nature. The nature is manifested in the inclinations. While the nature is manifested in the inclinations and the inclinations are naturally apprehended by human reason as good, the nature of any being, and, hence, the inclinations derive ultimately from God, that is, from eternal law. The third related notion is the ascription of the nature of beings in the created world to the activity of God. The will of God, the free creative act of God, is the ultimate source of that nature. The fourth related notion is that acts which are contrary to nature are opposed to the natural law and ultimately opposed to eternal law. The representative texts of Aquinas which elucidate these aspects of the natural law theory are the following. Of eternal law as the rule and measure of the created world in its relationship to God, Aquinas says,

> Just as in every artificer there pre-exists a type of the things that are made by his art, so too in every governor there must pre-exist the type of the order of those things that are to be done by those who are subject to his government. ... Now God, by His Wisdom,

is the Creator of all things in relation to which He stands as the artificer to the products of his art ... Moreover He governs all the acts and movements that are to be found in each single creature ... Wherefore as the type of the Divine Wisdom inasmuch as by It all things are created, has the character of art, exemplar or ideas; so the type of Divine Wisdom, a moving all things to their due end, bears the character of law. Accordingly the eternal law is nothing else than the type of Divine Wisdom, as directing all actions and movements (Aquinas, *Summa theologiae* I-II, q. 93, a. 1).

Of eternal law in its relationship to the world of nature, the world of created beings, Aquinas says,

There are two ways in which a thing is subject to the eternal law ... first by partaking of the eternal law by way of knowledge; second by way of action and passion, i.e. by partaking of the eternal law by way of an inward motive principle: and in this way, irrational creatures are subject to the eternal law ... But since the rational nature, together with that which it has in common with all creatures has something proper to itself inasmuch as it is rational, consequently it is subject to the eternal law in both ways; because while each rational creature has some knowledge of the eternal law ... it also has a natural inclination to that which is in harmony with the eternal law ... (Aquinas, *Summa theologiae* I-II, q. 93, a. 6).

Human beings, because they are rational beings are subject to the eternal law in two ways. They have a nature which has inclinations which press for actualization. The actualization of these inclinations is perfective of human nature. Hence, human beings may be said to be ruled and measured by that nature. However, they also have, as part of that human nature, intellect and will. The intellect and will rule and measure that nature by knowing it as it is manifest in the inclinations and commanding the accomplishment of the inclinations as perfective of that nature.

In regard to the human stewardship of the created world, the encyclical repeats the traditional view that the individual person has limited dominion over the body and limited dominion over the faculties of the body. In exercising stewardship, the individual person is allowed the use of the faculties and powers of the body and soul in accord with the immanent finality of the faculties or powers in the service of the life of the person. The destruction or mutilation of any faculty or power, whose finality is limited to the individual person, requires the application of the principle of totality. The destruction or mutilation of a faculty, for example, the generative faculty, whose finality lies beyond the individual person, requires the application of the principle of double effect prior to the application of the principle of totality. The notion of stewardship in this form was the achievement of Pope Pius XII. It represents his studied response to the intrusions of the totalitarian governments into the life and living of its citizens.

The claim of the encyclical regarding the sacredness of human life seems a twofold claim. The first claim is that human life is sacred. It has its origin in the creative power of God. The second claim is that the act itself in which human life is generated is sacred. It has its origin in the design of God.

Consequences for Reproductive Finality

From within the parameters defined by the intrinsic structure of the marriage act as expressive of the procreative potentiality and the unitive potentiality, by the inseparable unity of those potentialities, and by the other explicit principles operative in the tradition, including the natural law structure, the stewardship over the created world, and the sacredness of human life, *Humanae vitae* addresses the regulation of birth within marriage. Three kinds of acts are characterized as intrinsically evil acts and, as such, are specifically excluded as appropriate methods of birth regulation. They are direct abortion, direct sterilization, and direct contraception. Direct abortion, and any other action disruptive of the generative process which marks the continuum of human existence, continues to be recognized as the direct taking of innocent human life. In regard to direct abortion the encyclical says, "directly willed and procured abortion, even if for therapeutic reasons, is to be absolutely excluded as lawful means of birth regulation" (Paul VI 1968, 14).

Direct sterilization continues to be understood as the interference or the destruction of the immanent finality of the generative organs, which have ends beyond the individual. Inasmuch as these organs have finality beyond the physical integrity of the person, the encyclical pro-scribes direct sterilization, whether that sterilization be temporary or permanent, of either marital partner. The principle of totality, within limits defined by the principle of double effect, governs the moral determination of the act of direct sterilization. The limits set forth in the application of the principle of double effect are the following. First, the action itself is good or indifferent. Second, the good effect is not produced by means of the bad effect. Third, only the good effect and not the bad effect is directly intended. Fourth, there is a proportionate reason for placing the action and permitting the bad effect. Sterilization as a medical or surgical procedure, necessary to serve the good of the person, in the presence of threat to life or health, is permitted. Sterilization as a method of conception limitation is not permitted. In regard to this last type of activity, the bad effect, direct contraception, is directly intended and the good effect, conception regulation, is accomplished by the sterilizing procedure.

Direct contraception continues to be assessed as an intrinsically evil act. It is defined as any act which would render conjugal intercourse intentionally infertile. Direct contraception opposes the natural finality of the organs of generation and it opposes the inseparable connection between the unitive capacity and the procreative capacity of the conjugal act. An act which deprives a particular actualization of intercourse of its procreative power, whether the act of privation be accomplished prior to, simultaneous with, or following the act of intercourse, is assessed as an inappropriate means of conception regulation. The specification of the privative act by time seems directed to the exclusion of any means whether the deprivation be accomplished by mechanical, behavioral, or chemical means. Whether the privative act is intended as an end in itself or as a means to some other end, which end may be good in itself, the act is considered as directly contraceptive. The focus here is on direct contraception as a direct action which interferes with a good of the conjugal act. The encyclical says,

> In truth, if it is sometimes licit to tolerate a lesser moral evil in order to avoid a greater evil or to promote a greater good, it is not licit, not even for the gravest reason, to do evil in order that good may follow therefrom. One may not ... make into the object of a positive act of the will something that is intrinsically disordered and

hence unworthy of the human person, even when the intention is
to safeguard or promote individual, family or social goods (ibid.).

The evaluation of contraception as an intrinsically evil act and the
application of the inseparability principle, that is, the indissoluble
connection between the procreative significance and the unitive significance of every conjugal act, provide the frame for fashioning the
response to the Majority Report of the Special Pontifical Commission.
The Majority Report that issued from the theologians included the
assessment that the actualization of the procreative potentiality be
understood as a requirement of the entire course of the marriage
rather than a requirement of every single act of intercourse within the
marriage. The Majority Report argues that the moral specification of
marriage, considered as an act in itself, derives not from particular
acts which constitute partial aspects of the marriage but from the set
of acts throughout the duration of the marriage. The Majority Report
says, "Infertile conjugal acts constitute a totality with the fertile acts
and have a single moral specification" (Majority Report 1967, III).
The response of *Humanae vitae* is:

> And to justify acts made intentionally infertile one cannot invoke
> as valid reasons the lesser evil, or the fact that when taken together
> with the fertile acts already performed or to follow later, such acts
> would coalesce into a whole and hence would share in one and the
> same moral goodness (Paul VI 1968, 14).

While *Humanae vitae* proscribes direct acts of abortion, contraception, and sterilization, the encyclical maintains the licitness of
indirect sterilization and the licitness of conception regulation accomplished by periodic abstinence. The position of *Humanae vitae* on
indirect sterilization is acknowledged to be built on norms developed
by Pius XII. It allows for sterilization in the presence of disease or in
the danger of disease in specifically systemically related organs under
the governance of the principle of totality limited by the principle of
double effect. The application of these principles requires that the
intention of the sterilizing procedure be the cure or abatement of the
related disease and not the incapacitation of the procreative potentiality.

Contraception regulation achieved through the limitation of conjugal intercourse to the infertile phase of the fertility cycle of the woman is viewed by the encyclical as aligning human activity with the ordinance of Eternal Law. The encyclical says,

> [I]t is then licit to take into account the natural rhythms immanent in the generative functions and to make use of marriage during the infertile times only, and in this way to regulate births without offending the moral principles that we have already recalled (ibid., 16).

The encyclical recognizes again the distinction between acts of conjugal intercourse that are deliberately chosen in which it is impossible to actualize the procreative finality because of naturally occurring infertility in the woman and acts of conjugal intercourse in which it is impossible to actualize the procreative finality because of the specific choices of the spouses to employ means to actualize infertility. The former are permitted; the latter are proscribed. The critical difference according to the document is that while the intention remains the same in each instance, that is, to have intercourse as expressive of the unitive tendency but to avoid conception, in the latter instance a natural process is deliberately impeded, while in the former there is no direct interference. This position is grounded in an interpretation of natural law in which biological processes are viewed as controlling. It receives supplemental support from other arguments in the text. One is that by limiting conception regulation to periodic abstinence the faithfulness of marriage is protected. Another is that the natural method of conception regulation serves to enhance the proper ordering of love within marriage.

Following the assessment of direct acts of abortion, sterilization, and contraception as intrinsically evil, *Humanae vitae* warns of possible deleterious effects as the consequence of violating the principles of the tradition in regard to the regulation of birth. The consequences, which the encyclical maintains should be evident to responsible and reasonable human beings, are several. The first danger is the decline in sexual morality in general brought about by the increase in infidelity and premarital sex made probable by the removal of the risk of procreation in extramarital intercourse. The second is the threat to the dignity of the wife brought about by the failure to respect her psychic and physical equilibrium, which the encyclical expresses as "*corporis animaque aequilibritate*" (ibid., 17). The loss of respect transforms the status of the wife from loving consort to that of an object to be used for sexual gratification. The third is the danger of the adoption of these intrinsically evil methods of birth regulation as governmental policies for the resolution of procreative related problems whether those problems be individual, familial, societal or global. The fourth is the danger that the operative mentality of the human person in the solution of pressing human problems will shift from stewardship of the body and the organs of the body in the service of the intrinsic value of the person to that of domination of the body and its organs consequent on a mechanical assessment of the body and its organs as spare parts.

Summary of *Humanae vitae*

In summary, the essential nature of marriage, as it emerges from the text of *Humanae vitae* is that of a procreative union. This understanding represents a shift from the understanding of the essential nature of marriage as a procreative institution as found in *Casti connubii* and the earlier addresses of Pius XII. While the unitive aspect appears in embryonic form in *Casti connubii* and in the earlier allocutions of Pius XII, the unitive aspect begins to exercise any real controlling influence with the later allocutions which addressed the question of artificial insemination. The nature of marriage as a procreative union is manifested in the particular human act which is reserved to marriage. That act is conjugal intercourse. Conjugal intercourse, as described in *Humanae vitae*, has two distinct but inseparable ends. The encyclical designates these ends as the procreative aspect and the unitive aspect. Parity of ends rather than hierarchy of ends is the claim. The additional claim of inseparability of ends requires that each conjugal act be expressive of both ends. The unitive end is expressive of love. It unites husband and wife. In its instantiation in conjugal intercourse, it signifies, intensely, although relatively briefly, the personal union of the spouses. In addition, the actualization of the union is efficacious in the flourishing of the union. The procreative end of conjugal intercourse is expressive of a special fecundity, children. In its ordination to the existence and nurturing of children, it transforms husband and wife into parents. Its instantiation unites them to the creative activity of God. The encyclical maintains that each act of conjugal intercourse must be expressive of both proper ends. To engage in an act of intercourse which deliberately suppresses the unitive significance or which deliberately suppresses the procreative significance is to directly act against the good of marriage.

The encyclical maintains that an act of intercourse which directly suppresses either aspect of the conjugal act is an intrinsically evil act. The determination that such acts are intrinsically evil follows from the ethical theory that provides the foundation for the argumentation. The essential elements in that ethical theory are, first, the objective characterization of a human act as good or evil in its nature and, second, the determination of the object of the act as good or evil. In the first, the determination of an act as intrinsically evil, the controlling notion is the objective aspect of the act. If the objective aspect of the act is evil, neither the goodness of the intention nor the goodness of the circumstances, can change the characterization of the act as evil. The interference with the reproductive finality, from within the ambit of concerns addressed by *Humanae vitae*, provides an example. If the suppression of the procreative aspect is, in its objective characterization, an evil act, then neither compelling circumstances, such as poverty or illness, nor compelling reasons, such as the intention to exercise responsible parenthood, can alter the specification of the act as intrinsically evil.

In the second, the determination of the objective aspect of a human act as intrinsically evil, the natural law theory is the controlling element. In *Humanae vitae*, the operative natural law theory is one that emphasizes, in the proximate derivation of natural law, nature, the ontological element, over reason, the gnoseological element, and one that gives primacy in the remote source of natural law to its determination in the will of the Creator. In regard to the derivation of natural law, the proximate derivation is the accomplishment of the instrumentality of human reason as it reflects on human nature. Human reason naturally apprehends in the inclinations that are manifestations of human nature the goods or ends whose accomplishment is perfective of that nature. Human reason directs the pursuit of these goods in the proper circumstances and for the proper reasons. The ontological element is the set of ends that define the essential constitution of the human person. The gnoseological element is the activity of practical reason which governs the accomplishment of the inclinations of human nature in circumstances which are appropriate and for reasons that are properly ordered. The ontological element as described by Jacques Maritain is "an order or disposition which human reason can discover and according to which the human will must act in order to attune itself to the essential and necessary ends of the human being" (Maritain 1988, 205). The emphasis on the ontological element is evident within the text of *Humanae vitae* as the determinant of the meaning of the conjugal act is controlled by the biological processes of the organs of generation rather than controlled by the integral good of the person or the good of the marriage. The natural processes are assessed as the design of God and, as such, are considered morally normative. Several examples of the emphasis on biologism from the text itself are the following. In section 10, the text reads, "human reason discovers in the power of giving life biological laws which are pertinent to the human person." In section 11, the encyclical says, "God has wisely arranged natural laws and rhythms of fertility which of themselves bring about a separation in the succession of births." In section 12, the intrinsic structure of the conjugal act is governed by "laws inscribed in the very being of man and woman." In section 13, the transmission of human life in an act of mutual love is said to be "according to particular laws, inserted therein ... [in accord] ... with the design constitutive of marriage, and the will of the Author of life." Section 13 continues with the statement that the use of the gifts of God in a manner which negates, even if only partially, the significance of the gifts is to "act contrary to the nature of both man and woman and of their most intimate relationship." It reiterates the same emphasis on the physiological structure as controlling with the requirement that those who engage in conjugal love respect the "laws of the generative process." In section 16, direct contraception is proscribed as an act which impedes the "working of a natural process," and acceptable regulation of conception is accomplished by taking into "account the natural rhythms immanent in the generative functions."

The remote source of natural law from within the tradition and from within *Humanae vitae* as an expression of the tradition is eternal law. Eternal law is described by Aquinas as the "the very idea of the government of things in God the Ruler of the universe" (Aquinas, *Summa theologiae* I-II, q. 91, a. 1). Eternal law is the design of God for the created world. In describing this plan Aquinas says,

> Therefore just as the plan of divine wisdom in accordance with which all things are created by it has the character of an art, or exemplar, or idea, so the plan of divine wisdom moving all things to their appropriate ends has the quality of law. Accordingly, the eternal law is nothing else than the rational plan of divine wisdom considered as directing all actions and movements (Aquinas, *Summa theologiae* I-II, q. 93, a. 1).

In the development of eternal law theory in the text of Aquinas, there appears to be a primacy accorded the intellect of God. The natural world exists as idea, plan, or exemplar in the eternal law. From this it would seem to follow that to know anything about the nature of the created thing is to know something of the idea of God of that thing. In the encyclical, Paul VI develops the natural law theory with the dependence on eternal law. However, the emphasis in the encyclical is on the will of God rather than the intellect of God. There are frequent references in the text of *Humanae vitae* to the will of God as the source of the laws of nature. Several examples of this emphasis on the will of God as the source of natural law from the text itself are the following. In section 4, natural law is said to be "an expression of the will of God." In Section 12, the indissoluble connection between the procreative aspect and the unitive aspect of conjugal intercourse is said to be "willed by God." Section 13 reiterates the inseparable connection principle as the "will of the Author of life." This emphasis on the will of God would seem to make human beings dependent, not on the apprehension of human nature by human reason for knowledge of human ends, but rather on the apprehension of the divine will. The encyclical maintains that it is the privileged task of the Church to transmit, interpret, and teach the commands of God. As a consequence it would seem that knowledge of the content of natural law and assent to its teaching is possible only because of and from within a faith context. This understanding seems consonant with the pastoral directive within the encyclical to priests that their submission to the teachings of *Humanae vitae* is required "not only for the reasons adduced, but more on account of the light of the Holy Spirit" (Paul VI 1968, 28).

Donum vitae

Introduction

The Vatican document, *The Instruction on Respect for Human Life in its Origin and on the Dignity of Procreation*, was prepared by the Congregation for the Doctrine of the Faith under the direction of its Prefect, Joseph Cardinal Ratzinger. The instruction, hereinafter referred to as *Donum vitae*, was received, approved, and ordered promulgated by Pope John Paul II on February 22, 1987. In the presence of advancing technologies directed to enhancing the accomplishment of the reproductive finality, *Donum vitae*, in its introduction, sets out the fundamental moral principles of the tradition that are to govern the use of these scientific advances. This is followed, in three parts, by the application of these principles to the specific problems encountered in the field of reproductive intervention technology. Part I, which applies the principle of the sacredness of human life to the human being from the first moment of existence, addresses the problems associated with the appropriate treatment to be accorded the human embryo. Part II, which applies the principles regarding the special nature of human procreation, addresses the problems associated with the scientific interventions in the process of procreation. Part III, which treats the relationship between civil law and moral law, offers direction in regard to appropriate legislation to protect existing human life and to protect the special institutions whose role is to transmit human life.

Because the principles contained in the introduction and the application of these principles to the accomplishment of the procreative finality as developed in Part II have significance for the work at hand, these sections will be examined. This will be followed by the description, as found in *Donum vitae,* of the nature of marriage, the assessment of marital love, the specification of the ends of marriage, and the consequences for the accomplishment of the reproductive finality.

Principles

In its introduction, *Donum vitae* assesses the advances of science, issues a warning, identifies its intended audience, delineates its claims, and, from within this context, proffers the criteria that are to govern scientific procedures in the field of reproductive technology. In its positive assessment of science, *Donum vitae* views the advances of science as the actualization of the Genesis command that humanity bring the created world under its dominion. The warning contains the reminder that science and technology, which are recognized as human goods, can also, as the sad history of mankind offers ample testimony, be instruments of the domination of humanity. The document says,

> Basic scientific research and applied research constitute a significant expression of this dominion of man over creation. Science and technology are valuable resources for man when placed at his service and when they promote his integral development for the benefit of all; but they cannot of themselves show the meaning of existence and human progress (*Donum vitae* 1987, Intro., 2).

Within the parameters defined by the positive and negative assessments of science, *Donum vitae* recognizes the appropriateness, and even the good, of artificial interventions which serve the human good.

The intended audience for *Donum vitae* includes both those who are faithful to the tradition and those who, while outside the tradition, value the role of the tradition as an institution with a history of service to the human good.

The claims contained in the Introduction are that life is the gift of God to humanity and that the task of humanity, having received this gift, is its appropriate development. The description of the life that has been received is developed in terms of integral humanism. The core notion is that of the human person, who, while constituted of spiritual and corporeal elements, actualizes life as a unified whole integrating the elements that are constitutive of human life. The actualization of human life is said to be under the governance of natural moral law which, "expresses and lays down the purposes, rights and duties which are based upon the bodily and spiritual nature of the person" (ibid., 3). In an attempt to dissociate this interpretation of natural law from the biologism associated with the past of the tradition and, yet, to maintain the status of natural law as based on an objective order in the created world *Donum vitae* repeats the characterization of the natural law that is found in *Humanae vitae*. It says,

> [T]his law cannot be thought of as simply a set of norms on the biological level; rather it must be defined as the rational order whereby man is called by the creator to regulate his life and actions and, in particular, to make use of his own body (ibid.).

Natural law is neither reason alone nor nature alone. It is the result of the reflection of reason on nature, of the apprehension by reason of the goods of nature, and of the injunction of reason to accomplish the natural goods.

From within the natural law framework, enhanced by revelation and the past teachings of the tradition, *Donum vitae* maintains that life is a human good and that marriage has a specific nature as an institution created by God. In regard to the good that is life in its physical and personal dimensions *Donum vitae* says,

> Physical life, with which the course of human life in the world begins, certainly does not itself contain the whole of a person's value, nor does it represent the supreme good of man who is called to eternal life. However, it does constitute in a certain way the "fundamental" value of life, precisely because upon this physical life all the other values of the person are based and developed. The inviolability of the innocent human being's right to life "from the moment of conception until death" is a sign and requirement of the very inviolability of the person whom the Creator has given the gift of life (ibid., 4).

In regard to the specific nature of marriage, *Donum vitae* asserts that marriage is a calling to humanity as male and female to live life in a particular way. The nature of marriage specifies the goods and values that are to be realized within marriage. These goods and values are identified in the document as union and procreation. The document says,

> God who is love and life, has inscribed in man and woman the vocation to share in a special way in his mystery of personal communion and in his work as Creator and Father. For this reason marriage possesses specific goods and values in its union and in procreation which cannot be likened to those existing in lower forms of life (ibid., 3).

In regard to the procreative good, *Donum vitae* maintains the special character of the transmission of human life. The document in repeating a notion found in the 1961 encyclical letter, *Mater et magistra*, of Pope John XXIII says,

> [T]he transmission of human life has a special character of its own, which derives from the special nature of the human person. "The transmission of human life is entrusted by nature to a personal and conscious act and as such is subject to the all-holy laws of God: immutable and inviolable laws which must be recognized and observed. For this reason one cannot use means and follow methods which could be licit in the transmission of the life of plants and animals" (ibid., 4).

In its Introduction, *Donum vitae* offers no specific treatment of the good of the union.

The criteria that emerge from the introduction to form the operative principles of the document are, first, the respect for human life, and, second, respect for the special nature of the transmission of human life. In regard to the respect to be accorded human life, the principle enunciated by *Donum vitae* says, "God alone is the Lord of Life from its beginning until its end; no one can, in any circumstance, claim for himself the right to destroy directly an innocent human being" (ibid., 5). In regard to the respect for the special nature of the transmission of human life, the document building on the conciliar document *Gaudium et spes* says,

> Human procreation requires on the part of the spouses responsible
> collaboration with the fruitful love of God; the gift of human life
> must be actualized in marriage through the specific and exclusive
> acts of husband and wife, in accordance with the laws inscribed in
> their persons and in their union (ibid.).

It is this latter principle that governs the resolution of questions
regarding the appropriate means of accomplishing the reproductive
finality found in Part II of *Donum vitae*. Its more complete expression
emerges in a set of increasingly more specific principles in the treatment of the different reproductive procedures possible within the
contemporary medical-technical horizon. These procedures include
heterologous artificial fertilization and insemination, homologous artificial fertilization and insemination, embryo transfer, and surrogate
motherhood.

Development/Application of the Principles

The first of the more specific principles states that the accomplishment of procreation is appropriate only within marriage. The
Instruction says, "from the moral point of view a truly responsible
procreation vis-à-vis the unborn child must be the fruit of marriage"
(*Donum vitae* II, A, 1). The second principle states that the accomplishment of procreation is appropriate only within the partnership of
the marriage. *Donum vitae* says, "the bond existing between husband
and wife accords the spouses, in an objective and inalienable manner,
the exclusive right to be father and mother solely through each other"
(ibid., A, 2). The third principle maintains that the accomplishment
of procreation is appropriate only within the specific act of conjugal
intercourse, an act which carries the inseparable meanings of procreation and union. The fourth principle states that only procreation
accomplished within conjugal intercourse carries with it the dignity
appropriate to the origin of human life.

The first principle, procreation within marriage, and the second
principle, procreation limited to the partners of the marriage, have
a long history within the tradition. In addition, these notions, as an
expression of spousal commitment and procreative responsibility, are

widely respected in other traditions (Davitt 1978, 50ff.). In enunci-
ating the first principle, *Donum vitae* evaluates procreation as the
specific representation of the giving of the spouses to one another. The
second principle assesses procreation as an expression of the faithfulness
of the spouses to each other. Both these principles are regarded as efficacious in serving the triple goods of the child, the parents, and the
society. In regard to the good of the child, the document says, "it is
through the secure and recognized relationship to his own parents that
the child can discover his own identity and achieve his own proper
human development" (*Donum vitae*, II, A, 1). In regard to the good
of the parents, *Donum vitae* says,

> The parents find in the child a confirmation and completion of their
> reciprocal self-giving: the child is the living image of their love, the
> permanent sign of their conjugal union, the living and indissoluble
> concrete expression of their paternity and maternity (ibid.).

And in regard to the good of society, the instruction says,

> By reason of the vocation and social responsibilities of the person,
> the good of the children and of the parents contributes to the good
> of the civil society; the vitality and stability of society require that
> children come into the world within a family and that the family
> be firmly based on marriage (ibid.).

The third principle, that of the inseparable connection between
the procreative aspect and the unitive aspect in every act of conjugal
intercourse, has emerged, in this explicit formulation, only recently in
the tradition. In addition to the testimony of the recent documents of
the tradition, *Donum vitae* claims that the foundation of the principle
is to be found in the nature of marriage and in the connection of the
several goods of marriage. The examination of the foundation of the
inseparability principle proceeds, first, with the exposition of its roots
in the rather recent documents of the tradition and, then, with the
search for its grounding in the nature of marriage and the connection
of the goods of marriage as these appear in the other sources used by
the tradition to derive its canons.

The Inseparability Principle

In substantiating the claim of the inseparability principle, the instruction cites *Humanae vitae* of Pope Paul VI as the proximate source and an address by Pope Pius XII as the remote source in the tradition. In building on *Humanae vitae*, the instruction says,

> The church's teaching on marriage and human procreation affirms the "inseparable connection, willed by God and unable to be broken by man on his own initiative, between the two meanings of the conjugal act: the unitive meaning and the procreative meaning. Indeed, by its intimate structure, the conjugal act, while most closely uniting husband and wife, capacitates them for the generation of new lives, according to the laws inscribed in the very being of man and woman" (ibid., B, 4).

In building on the remote source, *Donum vitae* turns to an address by Pius XII to the participants in the Second Naples World Congress on Fertility and Sterility. In quoting Pius XII, *Donum vitae* says, "fertilization is licitly sought when it is the result of a 'conjugal act which is per se suitable for the generation of children to which marriage is ordered by its nature and by which the spouses become one flesh'" (ibid.). This is a representative statement from one of the addresses of Pius XII, who in the second half of his papacy was called on to resolve, in the presence of advances in human reproductive technology, the question of artificial insemination. The resolution of this problem, in these addresses, is accomplished by reference to marriage as a union. Artificial insemination is violative of the marital union. The inseparability principle, then, emerged in stages. The union as a distinct, yet, controlling element is the accomplishment of Pius XII. The inseparability of the procreative significance and unitive significance is explicitly claimed but not substantiated by Paul VI.

However, *Donum vitae* attends to the task, albeit in a limited fashion, of the validation of the inseparability principle. And, in keeping with the practice of the tradition, *Donum vitae* frames its defense, not in a positivist fashion of repeating prior claims, but as a development from a set of complementary and mutually correcting sources. This set of sources usually includes, in addition to the explicit statements of the tradition, meanings drawn from the privileged texts of the Scriptures, as well as direction and information from philosophy and the human sciences. Having presented those recent statements of the tradition, it is appropriate to examine those other sources, inasmuch as they appear in the instruction, for their special contributions in establishing the inseparability principle.

For its scriptural direction in regard to the nature of marriage and the connection of the goods of marriage, *Donum vitae* turns to the texts and commands of Genesis. The instruction says, "God created man in his own image and likeness: 'male and female he created them' (Gn 1:27), entrusting to them the task of 'having dominion over the earth' (Gn 1:28)." And further on the instruction repeats the words of Pope Pius XII in his *Address to the Midwives* which carries the "two in one flesh" theme of Genesis. *Donum vitae* says, "the proper nature of the act is the expression of the mutual gift which, according to the words of Scripture, brings about union 'in one flesh'" (ibid., B, 6). These Scriptural texts are carriers of meaning. Among them are the following. Humanity, as male and female, has been created in the image of God. As God creates and loves, so too men and women are empowered to create and love. As God rules over the created world, so too men and women are empowered to rule over the created world. Marriage is an institution created by God in which humanity as male and female form a union. Conjugal intercourse is the mutual gift of the spouses to each other. These themes contribute several elements to the controlling principle of *Donum vitae*. Included among those contributory elements are the following. Marriage is a union. Marriage is a heterosexual union. In loving and creating, here the special activity of procreating, the spouses imitate the activity of God. These elements would appear to contribute to the substantiation of the first and second of the more specific claims of the controlling principle, that is, marriage is procreative and marriage is a union. There appears to be a limited contribution to the third claim, that is, marriage has two ends, procreation and union. However, the limited contribution to the controlling principle is that procreation and union are inseparable from marriage not from each other. The Scriptural themes make no explicit contribution to that part of the third claim which maintains that both ends, procreation and union, are inseparable from each other and both are to be signified in every act of conjugal intercourse.

In establishing its operative principle from philosophical sources *Donum vitae* has recourse to natural law theory and integral humanism. In examining the philosophical sources, first, the structural elements provided by natural law theory and integral humanism, as they appear in *Donum vitae*, will be recalled. This will be followed by tracing the movement of the argument in the text of *Donum vitae*. In its explication of natural law theory, the instruction states,

> [T]his law cannot be thought of as simply a set of norms on the biological level; rather it must be defined as the rational order whereby man is called by the Creator to direct and regulate his life and actions and, in particular, to make use of his own body (ibid., Intro., 3).

Taking a position between competing philosophies of pure subjectivity, which views humanity as essentially will and reason, and pure physicalism, which views humanity as essentially material, whose resultant natural law notions are, respectively, reason only and nature only, *Donum vitae* maintains that natural law is derived from reason and nature. The role of reason is multifaceted. Reason reflects on nature which is a given as created by God. Reason apprehends the goods of nature as indicated by the inclinations, drives, or tendencies made manifest as the needs of nature. Reason commands the accomplishment of these goods. The relevant natures are those of marriage, "laws inscribed ... in their union" (ibid., 5), and of humanity, "laws inscribed in their persons" (ibid.) in its male and female presentations. The delineation of these natures is accomplished within the document only in terms of the structural elements of integral humanism. These elements are corporeality and spirituality. There is no attempt within the document to supply more specific content to this structure from appropriate sources in the relevant human sciences. The instruction maintains that human nature is neither purely corporeal nor purely rational. Humans live life as a unity constituted of spiritual and corporeal elements. Both elements are significant to the essential being that is human.

With the structural elements in place, the examination of the grounding of the inseparability principle as it appears in the document follows. This will be followed by an examination of the claims themselves. In substantiating the validity of the inseparability principle, the instruction maintains that the foundation of the linkage of meanings and goods derives from the substantial unity of the human person constituted of corporeal and spiritual elements in the service of the unified totality. *Donum vitae* says, "The moral value of the intimate link between the goods of marriage and between the meanings of the conjugal act is based upon the unity of the human being, a unity involving body and spiritual soul" (ibid., B, 4). The document utilizes two distinct claims to substantiate its inseparability principle. One is that marriage is a union similar to the substantial union of body and soul that characterizes the existence of the human person. The second is that, just as the human being expresses life in a fashion that integrates the corporeal and spiritual elements that constitute human life as personal, so too, marriage and the act of marriage are expressive of personal love which similarly integrates corporeal and spiritual elements. What would seem to follow would be the claim that marriage is a personal union within which certain goods as ends are to be accomplished. What, in fact, does follow in the instruction is the repetition of the inseparability principle as found in the language of Pope John Paul II. *Donum vitae* says,

> Spouses mutually express their personal love in the "language of the body," which clearly involves both "spousal meanings" and parental ones. The conjugal act by which the couple mutually express their self-gift at the same time expresses openness to the gift of life. It is an act that is inseparably corporeal and spiritual. It is in their bodies and through their bodies that the spouses consummate their marriage and are able to become father and mother. In order to respect the language of their bodies and their natural generosity, the conjugal union must take place with an openness to procreation; and the procreation of a person must be the fruit and result of married love (ibid.).

The claim that the conjugal act is a personal act, that is, both corporeal and spiritual, is unproblematic. The claim that the conjugal act which expresses spousal meaning and parental meaning has a physical element in its expression is also unproblematic. The move from the description of the conjugal act as "inseparably corporeal and spiritual" to the claim of the inseparability of the procreative aspect and the unitive aspect in every conjugal act is problematic.

Inseparability: A Problematic Claim

The task of examining the problematic claim follows. From the claim that marriage is a union similar to the substantial union of the body and the soul that characterizes the existence of the human person, it seems appropriate to develop the following analogy. Just as the corporeal and spiritual elements come together to form the unity that is the human organism, so too, the human being as male and the human being as female come together and generate a new entity, the marriage itself. However, since the constituting elements of each unity are different, the resultant unions are different. The union of body and soul results in an individual person. The union of man and woman results in a unified totality of two distinct but relating persons. It is a personal union. The differences in the nature of the organism generated by each set of ontologically different relating principles is not without significance.

In the past, the tradition has utilized the distinction between various types of unities considered as organisms as a limiting principle. The distinction between organisms as either a physical unity or a moral unity was developed by Pope Pius XII to govern the application of the principle of totality in the determination of the appropriateness of mutilating medical and experimental procedures. The distinction may be recalled from the works of Pope Pius XII as the following. Physical organisms are distinguished from moral organisms. An organism is a physical whole, if it has a unity subsisting in itself. It has unity on the level of essence. The relationship of part to whole exists, if the part as a member is an integral part of the physical unity. That is, if it

> [I]s an integral part destined by all its being to be inserted in the whole organism. Outside the organism it has not, by its very nature, any sense, any finality. It is wholly absorbed by the totality of the organism to which it is attached (Pius XII 1952 [44], 786).

A moral organism, for example a community, is a whole which is a union of individuals bound together for the realization of some common goal or action. The individuals who are members of a moral whole have meaning in themselves outside that determined by their role as collaborators in the common enterprise that unites the group. The moral organism has a unity on the level of action.

From the distinction of organisms as either physical or moral wholes, there follows the corresponding limitation of action in the application of the principle of totality. If the organism is a physical unit, then the extent of control over the parts is significantly different. The extent of this control is made specific by Pius XII in the following:

> The master and user of the organism ... can dispose directly and immediately of integral parts, members and organs within the scope of their natural finality. He can also intervene, as often as and to the extent that the good of the whole demands, to paralyze, destroy, mutilate and separate the members (ibid.).

On the other hand, if the organism is a moral unit, the application of the principle is limited to the activities of the members, not the physical being of the members, in the service of the whole.

The union of a man and a woman in marriage is a union of two distinct but relating persons. This union has similarities to both a physical union and a moral union. However, it is neither. It is a unique kind of union; it is an intimate personal union. In its "two in one flesh" reality, it accomplishes, by means of the organs of copulation, a physical union. However, as a personal union in which consciousness and conscience are engaged, it is always more than a physical union. In addition, conception results occasionally, not necessarily, from an act of conjugal intercourse. While a specific act of conjugal union might intend procreation, the accomplishment of procreation is distant both in time and space from the act of conjugal union. There is no insepa-rable connection, as an order discernible in the nature of the marriage act, between the unitive aspect and the procreative aspect of the act of conjugal intercourse. Inasmuch as procreation is distant in time and place from the unitive reality of marital intercourse, interventions, whether to avoid or to accomplish conception, which are distant in time and place are appropriate. In addition, the accomplishment of conception is dependent upon the integrity of the physical elements including the organs of reproduction, the germ cells, the routes of passage and the organ of implantation. The similarities of marriage to a moral unity are found in the establishment of the family. The family is the common enterprise that unites the group. However, the members, as unique and separate individuals, of the family have meaning outside the family. This limited defense of the inseparability principle is brought to closure without the material contributions from the human sciences, especially anthropology and psychology, and without reflection on the experience of the married.

Nonetheless, the inseparability principle is maintained and is joined by a new principle, that of the dignity of origin appropriate to the human person. This principle asserts that the personal dignity of the child requires that the child be the result of the act of the love and union of the parents, "the fruit of mutual giving which is realized in the conjugal act wherein the spouses co-operate as servants and not as masters in the work of the Creator who is Love" (*Donum vitae* II, B, 4). The child cannot be regarded as an object, the "product of an intervention of medical or biological techniques" (ibid.). *Donum vitae* maintains that it is not asserting a claim here for a non-existing subject. The claim that the document maintains that it is asserting is that the transmission of human life has a special character that must be respected. This position is made specific in a note in the instruction, which says,

> No one, before coming into existence, can claim a subjective right to begin to exist; nevertheless, it is legitimate to affirm the right of the child to have a fully human origin through conception in conformity with the personal nature of the human being. Life is a gift that must be bestowed in a manner worthy both of the subject receiving it and of the subjects transmitting it (ibid., note 32).

Consequences for Reproductive Finality

Having completed the exposition of the principles, the next task is the examination of the application of the principles. The application of these first two principles, procreation within marriage and procreation with the partners of the marriage, eliminates the accomplishment of the reproductive finality through heterologous artificial insemination or fertilization or any form of surrogacy as third party intrusion into the marriage partnership. This assessment is made explicit in the document. In regard to the use of ovum or sperm other than those of the marriage partners, *Donum vitae* says,

> Recourse to the gametes of a third person, in order to have sperm or ovum available, constitutes a violation of the reciprocal commitment of the spouses and a grave lack in regard to that essential property of marriage which is unity (ibid., II, A, 2).

Here third party intervention is a material intervention. The first and second principles are joined by the fourth principle in the rejection of surrogate motherhood. The instruction says,

> Surrogate motherhood represents an objective failure to meet the obligations of maternal love, conjugal fidelity and responsible motherhood; it offends the dignity and right of the child to be conceived, carried in the womb, brought into the world and brought up by his own parents; it sets up, to the detriment of families, a division between the physical, psychological and moral elements which constitute those families (ibid., II, A, 3).

The gestational role of surrogacy is a third party intervention that may be described as both material and instrumental.

The inseparability principle is added to the other three principles to provide the framework for *Donum vitae* to develop its conclusions which govern technical assistance in the accomplishment of the reproductive finality within the partnership of marriage. The first conclusion assesses homologous in vitro fertilization and embryo transfer; the second assesses homologous artificial insemination. In regard to homologous in vitro fertilization and embryo transfer, *Donum vitae* holds that it is inappropriate if "brought about outside the bodies of the couple and through the action of third parties whose competence and technical activity determine the success of the procedure" (ibid., II, A, 5). This disapproval of homologous in vitro fertilization and embryo transfer derives from the following five reasons. First, it is accomplished outside the body. Second, it is violative of the principle which excludes third party intervention. Here the third party intervention is an instrumental intervention. Third, it is assessed as an act which instantiates the dominion of technology over human goods rather than the service of technology in the accomplishment of human goods. Fourth, it is violative of the inseparability principle which requires that procreation be accomplished in a specific act of spousal union. In the language of *Donum vitae*, procreation must be accomplished in "the conjugal act specific to the love between the spouses" (ibid., II, B, 5). And fifth, it is violative of the special dignity of the transmission of life principle. *Donum vitae*, says,

> Such fertilization is neither in fact achieved nor positively willed as the expression and fruit of a specific act of conjugal union. In homologous IVF and ET, therefore, even if it is considered in the context of '*de facto*' existing sexual relations, the generation of the human person is objectively deprived of its proper perfection: namely, that of being the result and fruit of a conjugal act in which the spouses can become "cooperators with God for giving life to a new person" (ibid., II, B, 5).

This negative assessment of homologous in vitro fertilization and embryo transfer is claimed to follow from the consideration of the procedure from within the framework defined by the set of mutually correcting and complementary sources, including scripture, tradition, philosophy, and anthropology. While its disapproval as a violation of the principles enunciated in the very recent documents of the tradition is evident within the instruction, the contribution of the other components of the set of sources is not so evident. For example, in regard to the first reason for the negative assessment of the procedure, *Donum vitae* accords, despite prior claims of operating within a framework of integral humanism, controlling status to the bodies of the spouses. In addition, in spite of its assessment of marriage as a personal union, it accords controlling status to marriage as a physical union. The transition in the understanding of the nature of marriage from a physical union to a personal union, accompanied by a more complete delineation of the essential characteristics of this personal union, and the application of this new understanding to the procedure of homologous in vitro fertilization and embryo transfer would seem to require a new assessment of the procedure and those serving the procedure.

The second consequence of the application of the principles developed in *Donum vitae* is the assessment of homologous artificial insemination as appropriate within marriage if "the technical means is not a substitute for the conjugal act but serves to facilitate and to help so that the act attains it natural purpose" (ibid., II, B, 6). The requirement is that procreation be related to the specific unitive act. *Donum vitae* does not offer any concrete examples of appropriate interventions. The document brings to closure its evaluation of the various procedures to accomplish the reproductive finality with two reminders. The first is to the medical profession: that they be respectful of the special nature of human procreation. The second is to married couples: that they be aware that their commitment to the marriage vocation carries with it the right to engage in conjugal intercourse, but not the right to a child. The instruction says,

> A true and proper right to a child would be contrary to the child's dignity and nature. The child is not an object to which one has a right, nor can he be considered as an object of ownership: rather, a child is a gift, "the supreme gift" and the most gratuitous gift of marriage, and is a living testimony of the mutual giving of his parents. For this reason, the child has the right, as already mentioned, to be the fruit of the specific act of the conjugal love of his parents; and he also has the right to be respected as a person from the moment of his conception (ibid., II, B, 8).

Summary of *Donum vitae*

In summary, the significant claims that emerge from *Donum vitae* are as follows. Marriage has an essential nature as an institution created by God. Marriage is a heterosexual union. Bisexuality is intended by God as a calling to humanity as male and female to love in a specific way, that is, to "personal communion" (ibid., Intro., 3), and to procreate, that is, "to share … in his work as Creator and Father" (ibid.). Union and procreation, then, are designated as the specific goods that are the ends of marriage. The goods of marriage, as well as the values and meanings, are regarded as personal. As personal goods, they are to be realized in a manner which integrates the corporeal and spiritual elements that are constitutive of human life.

In general, the conclusions of *Donum vitae* derive from its assessment of the nature of marriage as a procreative union. This essential nature of marriage is signified in the human act which is reserved to marriage. That act is conjugal intercourse. Conjugal intercourse, as described in *Donum vitae*, has two inseparable ends, procreation and union. Both of these ends must be signified in every act of intercourse within marriage. While the inseparability principle in itself is vulnerable, it is maintained by the document and it governs the resolution of the problems addressed in the instruction. As a consequence, homologous in vitro fertilization, some instances of artificial insemination, and direct contraception are assessed as inappropriate. Acts of conjugal intercourse which are directly contraceptive are opposed to the procreative meaning of the conjugal act. *Donum vitae* says of direct contraception that it, "deliberately deprives the conjugal act of its openness to procreation and in this way brings about a voluntary dissociation of the ends of marriage" (ibid., II, B, 4). The accomplishment of procreation outside a specific conjugal act expressing the unitive meaning of intercourse is similarly opposed to the meaning of the conjugal act. *Donum vitae* says, "from the moral point of view, procreation is deprived of its proper perfection when it is not desired as the fruit of the conjugal act, that is to say, the specific act of the spouses' union" (ibid.). Here *Donum vitae* reasserts a claim that is maintained in *Humanae vitae* in its assessment of contraceptive intercourse. That claim is the requirement that the procreative and the unitive meaning be signified in every single act of intercourse within the marriage, rather than the understanding that particular acts of intercourse within marriage are partial aspects of the vocation that is marriage. Operating from within the ambit of that same claim, *Donum vitae* requires that if procreation is to be accomplished, its accomplishment cannot be separated from the specific act of union. The moral determination of homologous in vitro fertilization and embryo transfer, as well as that of artificial insemination, cannot be derived from the totality that is the marriage vocation. The moral determination of any act must be made in reference to each single act of conjugal intercourse. And each act of conjugal intercourse must signify union and procreation.

In regard to the accomplishment of the reproductive finality in marriage the specific significant conclusions of *Donum vitae* are the following four. First, heterologous artificial fertilization is forbidden. Second, surrogate motherhood is forbidden. Both of these involve third party intrusion into the union of the marriage partners. Third, the procedure of homologous artificial fertilization and embryo transfer is forbidden. This negative assessment of homologous in vitro fertilization and embryo transfer is claimed to be an instance of third party intrusion into the union of the marriage partners. In addition, it is accomplished outside the bodies of the marriage partners. Furthermore, it is violative of the inseparability principle. And it is an instance in which technology dominates rather than serves the human good. Finally, it is violative of the principle of the special dignity of the transmission of human life. Fourth, homologous artificial insemination is permitted provided that the procedure is one that facilitates the accomplishment of the natural purpose of the conjugal act.

Chapter 3

The Tradition:
the Emerging Position

Shifting Profiles:

The Nature of Marriage/the Role of Conjugal Intercourse

The twentieth century has witnessed the transition from the specification of the essential nature of marriage as a procreative institution
to the understanding of marriage as a procreative union. From within
the context of marriage as a procreative institution, the exercise of
conjugal intercourse is governed primarily by the actualization of
the procreative end of marriage. This understanding lies in the long
shadow of the Augustinian tradition as found in the expression "con-
cubitus propter solam procreationem." This strict understanding could
not even be sustained by Augustine who yielded to the qualification
that intercourse without procreation be permitted in marriage as the
rendering of the debt in the remediation of concupiscence and in
the service of the marriage. In the modern era, this understanding
begins to give way in *Casti connubii* with the explicit recognition of
marriage as an intimate union and the explicit recognition of the role
of conjugal intercourse, not as a sin needing to be excused, but, as a
good in nourishing the union. While the primary end of marriage
remains procreation, approbation was accorded, for the first time,
to the exercise of intercourse directed to the accomplishment of the
secondary ends in themselves. Moreover, in this realization of the
secondary ends, the primary end may be intentionally excluded. The

singular restriction placed on the exercise of conjugal intercourse in the service of secondary ends was that nothing be done to vitiate the natural act. The requirement in *Casti connubii* is that "the intrinsic nature of the act be preserved" (Pius XI 1941, 59). This requirement, which evidences the influence of Franciscus Hurth, S.J., is to be understood as (1) the claim that the natural order and the moral order coincide and (2) the claim that conjugal intercourse is, in its nature, a reproductive act (McCormick 1989, 156-57).

This understanding carried over into the early part of the pontificate of Pope Pius XII who reaffirmed the essential nature of marriage as a procreative institution with emphasis on the procreative finality of marriage and emphasis on the immanent teleology of the reproductive organs beyond the individual. The primary end of marriage is still procreation. However, the Pontiff explicitly recognized that for a wide variety of prudential reasons, the reproductive finality may be avoided either permanently or temporarily in a particular marriage. The exercise of conjugal intercourse in the service of the secondary ends is permitted, and the primary end may be intentionally excluded in the act, indeed in every act of conjugal intercourse. In fact, it may be the case that the end designated as the primary end may never be accomplished within a particular marriage. The exercise of intercourse in the service of the secondary ends of the marriage is permitted under the same rubric as found in *Casti connubii*, that is, that "the intrinsic nature of the act be preserved" (Pius XI 1941, 59). In the latter part of the pontificate of Pius XII, in addressing the question of artificial insemination, in which the procreative good is accomplished outside a specific act of conjugal intercourse, the question is resolved in the presence of the understanding of marriage as a union of persons, rather than as a procreative institution. Artificial insemination is forbidden as violative of the personal, relational, unitive aspects of marriage. Procreation must be accomplished within the act of conjugal intercourse. If marriage were merely a procreative institution rather than a procreative union, then means to achieve procreation that were not unitive, for example, artificial insemination, would be permitted. Perhaps, they would even have been encouraged. However, that was not the case and with this treatment of artificial insemination, there begins the transition in the description of the essential nature of marriage.

Marriage begins to be considered a procreative union, with specific procreative and unitive ends, rather than a procreative institution.

A further transition in the understanding of marriage is found in the document of the Second Vatican Council, *Gaudium et spes*. This transition is the result of two shifts. The first is the shift in the foundation for moral judgments from the body as referent to the person, "integrally and adequately considered" (McCormick 1989, 14) as referent. The second is marked by the increased emphasis on responsible parenthood rather than simply reproduction as the procreative goal. In that document, it is marriage as the partnership of the couple, an intimate personal union, that serves as the core notion in the description of the essential nature of marriage. Marriage is described as "intimate partnership of married life and love" (*Gaudium et spes*, 48). The union, "rooted in the conjugal covenant of irrevocable personal consent" (ibid.) comes into existence with the consent of the partners to the marriage. In the intimate union that is marriage, conjugal intercourse is an act of persons. It is the act in which the "spouses mutually bestow and accept each other" (ibid., 50). The exercise of conjugal intercourse serves to nourish and sustain the union. Conjugal intercourse as an expression of marital love is valued in itself. It is into this intimate union of persons that children are to be born and nourished. Conjugal love is viewed as having an upward dispositive effect on the union to render the spouses of the union capable of sharing in the creative love of God. The exercise of conjugal intercourse is directed also, then, to the accomplishment of the end of children. Children are recognized as "the supreme gift of marriage" (ibid., 50). There remains, then, the ordination of marriage and conjugal love to children, but within the vocation of marriage as the accomplishment of responsible parenthood.

In *Humanae vitae*, marriage is characterized as a procreative union. It is the institution which accomplishes, in and through human activity, the plan of a loving God. This plan includes the end of the establishment and sustenance of the union and the end of the existence and nurturing of children. Parity of ends rather than hierarchy of ends is the overt claim. Marriage as a procreative union is described in the encyclical in the following:

By means of the reciprocal personal gift which is proper and exclusive to them, husband and wife tend toward that communion of their being whereby they help each other toward personal perfection in order to collaborate with God in the begetting and rearing of new lives (Paul VI 1968, 8).

The marital act, as the act which signifies the reality of marriage, is an act which is both procreative and unitive. The procreative meaning and the unitive meaning are inseparable. The encyclical maintains that there is an indissoluble connection between the unitive signification and the procreative signification of the conjugal act. Every act of conjugal intercourse must be expressive of both meanings, at least in the minimal fashion that there be no direct human intervention in the actualization of either meaning.

Donum vitae continues the understanding of marriage as a procreative union. Marriage is characterized as the institution created by God as a way for humanity as male and female to participate in the work and goodness of God. *Donum vitae* says, "God who is love and life, has inscribed in man and woman the vocation to share in a special way in his mystery of personal communion and in his work as Creator and Father" (*Donum vitae,* Intro., 3). Marriage as unitive is expressive of love as personal communion. Marital love is to be an emulation of God's love. Marriage as procreative expresses the creative power of humanity. It is an activity in which the marriage partners imitate and share in the work of creation. Conjugal intercourse as the sign of the essential nature of marriage must express both the unitive meaning and the procreative meaning. In building directly on *Humanae vitae,* *Donum vitae* maintains that every act of conjugal intercourse must signify both meanings. *Donum vitae* says,

> The church's teaching on marriage and human procreation affirms the "inseparable connection, willed by God and unable to be broken by man on his own initiative, between the two meanings of the conjugal act: the unitive meaning and the procreative meaning. Indeed, by its intimate structure, the conjugal act, while most closely uniting husband and wife, capacitates them for the generation of new lives, according to the laws inscribed in the very being of man and woman" (ibid., II, B, 4).

A New Profile:

The Nature of Marriage /the Role of Conjugal Intercourse

The examination of the tradition reveals a development in the explicitation of the essential nature of marriage as a consequence of the succession of approximate accounts of the essential nature of marriage. The progression in the understanding of the essential nature of marriage is accompanied by a corresponding transition in the understanding of the role of intercourse within marriage. The consequences of this partial understanding include an incomplete understanding of the role of intercourse in marriage and a disordered understanding of the place of reproductive finality within marriage. While the concrete accounts of the essential nature of marriage in the documents of the tradition in the past and the tradition in the present are incomplete, the heuristic structures are in place to guide the development of a more complete account of the essential nature of marriage. The examination of the documents of the tradition indicates that the tradition holds that marriage has an essential nature. It is a reality in the objective order. The tradition holds that sexual intercourse is the marriage act. It is a good within marriage. It signifies and contains the reality that is marriage. And its exercise is appropriate only within the marital union. The specification of the purpose of intercourse receives its determination from the specification of the essential nature of marriage. The essential nature of marriage, as a reality in the objective order, receives its specification not from the assessment of the act of intercourse based on the physiological structure of that act in the accomplishment of one of the ends of marriage, that is, not as an act of the nature that humanity has in common with the animals, but from a variety of sources, including revelation, natural law, theology, the teachings of the tradition, and the human sciences. Furthermore, the examination of the documents of the tradition reveals that the understanding of the essential nature of marriage has developed in history. The implicit has been made explicit over time.

The Emerging Position:

Marriage As an Intimate Personal Union

Having completed the examination of the documents of the tradition and having noted the partial accounts of the essential nature of marriage with the subsequent underdeveloped understanding of the function of intercourse within marriage and the effects of this partial account on the governance of the reproductive finality, the next task is the delineation of a more complete description of the nature and ends of marriage, the specification of the proper function of marital intercourse from the determination of the essential nature of marriage, and a consideration of the consequences of this more complete account on the moderation of the reproductive finality. While attempting to present a more complete sketch of the essential reality that is marriage, the attempt is recognized as still a profile. And the sketch remains open to development as knowledge increases and understanding grows to bring the features of the profile into sharper focus. The warrant for outlining a new profile derives from the tradition itself which claims a natural law foundation, more specifically natural law theory as presented by Saint Thomas Aquinas, for its position. In regard to that law Aquinas says, "Natural law is nothing else than the rational creature's participation of the eternal law" (Aquinas, *Summa theologiae* I-II, q. 92, a. 2). The minimal claims of the natural law theory of Thomas Aquinas are (1) there is order in the created world; (2) the order in the created world derives from eternal law; (3) the order in the created world is accessible to human reason; hence (4) there is an objective moral order accessible to human reason. The explication of any nature in the created world is accomplished, albeit never completely, in an empirical process. The process is directed by "the immanent and recurrently operative structure" (Lonergan 1964, xxvi) of human intelligence and results in the progressively cumulative set of judgments of concrete fact. The nature in question is examined in its concrete manifestations. The concrete manifestations are the inclinations and tendencies which press for actualization as perfections of the nature. From the experience and observations, an understanding of the nature is reached. In the presence of sufficient evidence the understanding is judged to be correct. In addition to the activity of reason which studies the nature, there is the activity of reason which seeks good. Practical reason in seeking goodness, as well as truth, recognizes the proper manner of the actualization of those tendencies and inclinations, and practical reason commands their realization. In the gift of nature and the gift reason and will, God gives to humanity the gift of self-government. Natural law precepts arise, not from a direct revelation from God, but in the grasp by human reason of the goods of human flourishing. Nothing, of course, prevents God from revealing to humanity those things which are required for their salvation and which, at least, some humans after a long time may come to know at least partially. An example of such activity is God's revelation of the Ten Commandments to Moses on Mt. Sinai.

Marriage: A Human Relationship

At present, the understanding has led to the emergence of a position that maintains that marriage has an essential nature as a particular type of human relationship. It is an intimate personal union. It is an intimate community of marital life and love. The union is promised, that is, it is ratified in an act of consent. The consent is signified, that is, initially and physically consummated in the normal course of events, in a particular type of act, the marriage act. The intimate relationship, as a singularity in being, a singularity in consciousness, and a singularity in conscience, is brought to completion, that is, more fully consummated, over a lifetime. The conjugal act most precisely signifies an intimate union which is marked by self-donation and self-acceptance. Marriage is, in its essential nature, an intimate union of persons. This intimate union in its personal aspects has been described in the following:

> The sexual intercourse of men and women is far more than the activity of their genital organs. It is more than physical and it is more than spiritual. It is a fusion of the two with each determining the other. Because of the spiritual component of the act it is the meeting of two persons. Indeed because of the intimate union with each of the persons of spirit and matter the sexual act can express the spiritual with exceptional force and clarity.

> In all other interactions of person and person they meet not
> "within" the act itself but in the middle-ground effects of each one's
> acts—for example, in art work, in speech, in teaching. But in sexual
> intercourse the persons meet within the act. Intercourse thus has a
> unique power for giving the self and accepting the other. And this
> power and function it has in and of itself, not from any symbol-
> ism added to it by the partners, not by any meaning coming to it
> from outside itself. The directness of bodily-spiritual expression in
> intercourse gives it a power to convey its meaning that surpasses
> all other human conveying of meaning (Mackin 1982, 232).

As a reality in the objective order, marriage is an entity constituted
in the real relation of subject to subject. The relationship, a union, is
established as a nexus or connection between two persons who are,
in their nature, mutually ordered to each other. The spouses, as the
principles of the relationship, are those whose "to be" precisely as
spouses is to be ordered to each other (Aquinas, *Summa theologiae*, I,
q. 28, a. 1). Each acts in the other; each is acted upon by the other.
The spouses are the related complementary principles of the being
that is the marriage. The marriage is a being in itself.

Just as the marriage, reified as the marriage bond, is the appropriate
juridical entity in canon law, that is, it has privileged standing in the
legal order, so too the marriage itself is the moral entity in the ethical
order. Actions of the related principles of the marriage, the spouses,
must be evaluated from within the context of the moral entity, the
marriage. It is the marriage, not the partners individually, not the
reproductive organs in isolation, that has privileged standing in the
moral order. As a union, the marriage is a personal relationship, a kind
of human friendship between a man and a woman, each embodying
a particular aspect of humanity. The union of sexually differentiated
persons instantiates ontological completeness. The relationship begins
on the horizontal plane as a consequence of attraction and desire on
the level of sensitive appetite. The essential nature of humanity as
male and female includes the inclination of each to desire the other in
such a way as to be united with the other. Because humanity, as male
and female, has a complex nature, that is, a nature that is physical,
appetitive, rational, and spiritual, the union has a similarly complex
nature that is physical, appetitive, rational, and spiritual. It is a union

of persons. It is a personal union that results in a bond that is more fully a union than a physical union. While the resultant personal unity has characteristics in common with both physical and moral unities, it is, in itself, a unique species of unity. The formation of the love directed union has been described by Dietrich von Hildebrand in his essay entitled "Marriage" in which he says,

> Their love tends to a unique union, even in part constitutes it, as a community where two persons constitute a closed union, which can exist only between them. Conjugal love constitutes a relationship in which the regard of each one of the two parties is turned exclusively upon the other (von Hildebrand 1942, 6).

The appetitive desiring and physical longing press for the actualization of the union. Because the union is more than a physical union, because the union must supply the conditions for the actualization and perfection of children, and because the union must serve as the condition for the perfection of the partners individually, the rational intercedes to govern the accomplishment of the union.

The union itself begins with the consent of each to establish a marriage, that is, a covenanted, lifelong, heterosexual, and sacramental union. The consent requires the desire and the antecedent capacity to bring to reality this union. This consent applies not only to the physical aspects of the union, but to all the aspects of the union considered as a life in common. The consent, as described by Theodore Mackin, S.J., in his work *What Is Marriage?*, is the consent along with the antecedent capacity to the following:

> (a) to the giving of themselves to one another for one another—and particularly as Christians to make the kind of mutual self-bestowal found in Christ's sacrificial love for the Church;
> (b) therefore to the forming of a covenant of love and fidelity …
> (c) therefore to the forming and maintaining of a communion of persons (Mackin 1982, 17).

The giving of consent marks the moment of the becoming of the marriage, that is, the *matrimoniun in fieri*. Following this consent the union itself, the *matrimonium in facto esse*, begins to emerge as a new being. This new being is explicitly recognized and accorded privileged standing in Canon Law as a juridical person, the marital bond. Initially, on the level of physical being, this union is generated and nourished in the conjugal act in which the two spouses become one flesh. In time the union that is marriage may realize not only the good life of human friendship, but the promised good of eternal life.

The understanding of marriage as essentially a union, while explicitly part of the revelation in the Scriptures, has a long, but somewhat neglected, history in the tradition. The reasons for the oversight are several, including the condition of the sciences as they relate to humanity and the limitation of perspective. Advances in the biological sciences, in the human sciences, and in the ethical perspective brought with them development of understanding. First, advances in the biological sciences brought with them a better understanding of the relationship between conjugal intercourse and reproduction. In both the Ancient and Medieval philosophers, reproduction was understood on the act-potency or matter-form model as an immediate effect of intercourse. The prevailing concept was that the male as active principle animated the material held passively by the female. Reproduction is known by contemporary science to be the result of syngamy in which both the male and female make significant contributions and to be distant in space and time from the act of conjugal intercourse. Second, the advances in the human sciences, especially psychology, brought with them a better understanding of the relationship between conjugal intercourse and the generation of the marital union as well as the effect of conjugal intercourse on the enhancement of the separate lives of the partners. The marital union is nourished by conjugal intercourse and the marital union determines the matrix of conditions which serve the maturation of the children of the marriage and the flourishing of the individual partners. Third, advances in ethics, especially in the ethical perspective, are being brought about by the participation in the ethical discussion of men and women, whose experience is the lived experience of the generation of the marital union and whose intellectual reflection is rooted in that concrete experience. From within a horizon enriched by these advances, it seems appropriate to examine that understanding of marriage as a union as elements of this characterization appear (1) in the Scriptures, (2) in the insights of philosophy, (3) in the recent documents of the tradition, and (4) in the contemporary commentary within the tradition.

Marriage As a Union in the Tradition

The Scriptures

Among the significant descriptions of the union in the Scriptures are the account of the two becoming one in Genesis, the reiteration of that account in the New Testament, and the Pauline characterization of marriage as the union which emulates the union of Christ and the church. The new union is the oneness spoken of in the Genesis description of the becoming and being of marriage. There it is said, "For this reason a man leaves his father and mother and clings to his wife, and the two shall become one flesh" (Gn. 2:18 22-24). The Scriptures of the New Testament reverberate with references to the Old Testament rendering of the marital union as two becoming one. In MATTHEW 19:5 and 6, the response of Jesus to the question of divorce contains the affirmation of the divine institution of marriage and of its effectuation of the oneness of man and woman in marriage. It is written:

> Jesus answered, "Haven't you read the scripture that says that in the beginning the Creator made people male and female? 'For this reason a man will leave his father and mother and unite with his wife, and the two will become one.' So they are no longer two, but one. Man must not separate, then, what God as joined together."

Paul also speaks of the two becoming one and refers to it as a deep, secret truth. He says in the letter to the Ephesians, 5:31-32,

> As the scripture says, "For this reason a man will leave his father and mother and unite with his wife and the two will become one." There is a deep secret truth revealed in this scripture, which I understand as applying to Christ and the Church. But it also applies to you: every husband must love his wife as himself, and every wife must respect her husband.

In addition, Paul, in Corinthians, 6:16, warns of the danger of intercourse with a prostitute as inappropriate instantiation of the union. He says, "perhaps you don't know that the man who joins his body to a prostitute becomes physically one with her."

Other elements that contribute to the fashioning of the unity, for example, singularity in consciousness and singularity in conscience emerge later. As a covenanted union it has the marks of faithful promise and sustaining love that reflect the covenant of redemptive love and fidelity between Christ and His church. As sacramental, it is a graced state, in which the grace renders the union indissoluble. This union, as is the case with all unions, has as an end the perfection of itself and the flourishing of the members of the union.

Philosophy Foundational for the Tradition

The understanding of marriage as a union is to be found in the philosophers whose insights are foundational for the tradition. Significant among those philosophers are Aristotle and Thomas Aquinas. In the *Nicomachean Ethics* and the *Politics*, Aristotle describes marriage. In addition to the description of marriage as the institution for reproduction and nurture of children, he offers several observations regarding the marital union itself. The first is that marriage is by nature a joining of two into oneness, that is, marriage is a *physei syndyastikon* (Aristotle 1941a, 1162a 16). Men and women are brought together in marriage by the natural impulse of sexual appetite. Second, the marital union is, as an institution prior to the civil community. This priority is temporal as well as necessary. Human beings are conjugal beings first and political beings only subsequently.
Aristotle says,

> Between other kinsmen friendly relations are found in due proportion. Between man and wife friendship seems to exist more by nature, for man is naturally inclined to form couples—even than to form cities, inasmuch as the household is earlier and more necessary than the city ... (ibid., 1162a 15-19).

Third, the marital relationship is described by Aristotle as a friendly relationship that is based on pleasure and utility and one which may even be a friendship founded on virtue. Aristotle describes this multifaceted relationship in the following:

> With the other animals the union extends only to this point, but human beings live together not only for the sake of reproduction but also for the various purposes of life; for from the start the functions are divided, and those of man and woman are different; so they help each other by throwing their peculiar gifts into the common stock. It is for these reasons that both utility and pleasure seem to be found in this kind of friendship. But this friendship may be based also on virtue, if the parties are good; for each has its own virtue and they will delight in the fact (ibid., 1162a20-27).

This passage carries the notion, not that people marry because they are friends, but rather, that the actualization of the natural biological relationship under the command of the rational may be conducive to the generation of a moral relationship, that is, the kind of friendship that is based on virtue.

The treatment of the nature of marriage by Saint Thomas Aquinas is found in the compilation that was taken from his *Commentary* on *Book IV* of *The Sentences* that is entitled "Supplement" to the *Summa theologiae* and in the third book of the *Summa contra gentiles*. In these synthetic accounts, which build on elements found in Aristotle, the Scriptures, and Augustine, Aquinas offers, in addition to the description of marriage as an institution for offspring and the remediation of concupiscence, observations of marriage as a natural relationship, a union between a man and a woman. This relationship, "a tie between the man and a definite woman" (Aquinas, *Summa theologiae*, Supplement, q. 41, a. 1), results from the combination of the action of the free will and the natural inclination of men and women to each other. In addition to the explicit description of marriage as essentially a heterosexual union, Aquinas designates two ends to be accomplished within marriage. They are a "principal end, namely the good of offspring ... existence, nourishment and education," and a "secondary end ... which is the mutual services which married persons render one another in household matters" (ibid.). In developing the definition of marriage, Aquinas defends the definition found in Distinction 27 of Book IV of the *Sentences of Peter Lombard*. The text of Peter Lombard defines marriage as "the marital union of man and woman involving their living together in individual partnership" (ibid., note p. 2724). In regard to that definition, Aquinas says,

> That definition given in the text indicates the essence of matrimony, namely the *union*, and adds determinate subjects by the words *between lawful persons*. It also points to the difference of the contracting parties in reference to the species, by the word *marital*, for since matrimony is a joining together for the purpose of some one thing, this joining together is specified by the purpose to which it is directed, and this is what pertains to the husband (*maritum*). It also indicated the force of this joining,—for it is indissoluble ... The remaining definition indicates the effect to which matrimony is directed, namely the common life in family matters (ibid., q. 44, a. 3).

In his characterization of the kind of joining that constitutes the union that is marriage, Aquinas describes marriage as a unity of purpose and a unity in being. In regard to a joining of purpose he says, "by marriage certain persons are directed to one begetting and upbringing of children, and again to one family life in respect of which we speak of husband and wife" (ibid., q. 44, a. 1). In regard to a joining in being, that is the bond, Aquinas maintains that the bond between the spouses is the reality contained in the marriage. He says, "the bond between husband and wife resulting from those acts is reality and sacrament; and the ultimate reality contained is the effect of the sacrament, while the non-contained reality is that which the Master [Peter Lombard] assigns" (ibid., q. 42, a. 1, ad 5). The reality signified but not contained in the marriage is the union of Christ with the church. Moreover, Aquinas notes the physical and spiritual aspects of the union which contribute to its constitution as a personal union when he says, "the joining together of bodies and minds is a result of matrimony" (ibid., q. 44, a. 1). And again, in describing the marital union, he says, "for the joining of husband and wife by matrimony is the greatest of all joinings, since it is a joining of soul and body, wherefore it is called a *conjugal* union" (ibid., q. 44, a. 2, ad 3). Because marriage is, in its essence, a joining together, Aquinas maintains that reference to marriage as a conjugal union is appropriate.

Furthermore, in the consideration of marriage as a relation, Aquinas maintains that every relation has a unity in the cause of the relationship and a diversity inasmuch as the subjects that are related in terms of that cause are diverse subjects. Now inasmuch as marriage has a unity of purpose and a unity of being, there is a cause that relates the diverse subjects in the unity of purpose and a cause that relates the subjects in the unity of being. In regard to the unity of purpose, the cause that relates the subjects is procreation. The diverse subjects are the man and the woman as potential parents. In regard to the unity of being, the cause that relates the subjects is the marriage bond. The diverse subjects are the man, as inclined to the woman, and the woman, as inclined to the man, as spouses.

In addition to the explicit references in these texts of Aquinas to marriage as, essentially, a union, other texts contribute to this claim and others yet disclose the reasons for the neglect of the union as the core notion. In regard to the latter, the failure to accord controlling status to the union may be partially accounted for as a residual effect of Stoicism and Augustinean Manichaeanism. In each of these traditions, there is found a suspicion in regard to the act of conjugal intercourse. This discomfort with the marriage act is evidenced in the treatment by Aquinas of the excusing of the act of conjugal intercourse by the attainment of the goods of marriage, namely, *proles, fides,* and *sacramentum.* Aquinas describes conjugal intercourse as an act accompanied by such powerful pleasure that reason is impaired. This impairment of reason by such exquisite pleasure, which pleasure Aquinas explicitly acknowledges as having been attached to the act of intercourse by Divine Providence, is assessed as a loss. The loss, however, is redeemed in the goods. Aquinas says, "the choice of this union cannot be made ordinate except by certain compensations whereby that same union is righted; and these are the goods which excuse marriage and make it right" (ibid., q. 49, a. 1).

Among the texts which contribute to the understanding of marriage as a union are those found in Book III of the *Summa contra gentiles.* For example in Chapter 123, which treats of marriage as indissoluble, Saint Thomas describes the role of friendship in sustaining the marital union and he describes the upward dispositive effect of conjugal intercourse in sustaining the marital union. He says,

> Furthermore, the greater the friendship is, the more solid and long-lasting will it be. Now there seems to be the greatest friendship between husband and wife, for they are united not only in the act of fleshly union, which produces a certain gentle association even among beasts, but also in the partnership of the whole range of domestic activity. Consequently, as an indication of this, man must even "leave his father and mother" for the sake of his wife, as is said in Genesis (2:24). Therefore it is fitting for matrimony to be completely indissoluble (Aquinas, *Summa contra gentiles* III, ch. 123, 6).

Moreover, he observes that the understanding of marriage as an indissoluble union serves not only the good of offspring but also the good of appropriate behavior of husband and wife. They will be more faithful in their love and more solicitous in the care of the household.

Recent Documents

The documents of the modern period, both those of the present and those of the immediate past, make reference to the union that is marriage. However, the union is not accorded controlling status in the determination of problems within the marriage. In *Casti connubii* the nature of marriage as an intimate union is affirmed in the words, "By matrimony ... the souls of the contracting partners are joined and knit together, more directly and intimately than are their bodies" (Pius XI 1941, 7). The text of *Casti connubii* records the longevity of the description of the essential nature of marriage as a union, from *Genesis* to Christ to Trent and reaffirms in the present that characterization of marriage. The encyclical in quoting the documents that issued from Trent says, "Christ our Lord very clearly taught that in this bond two persons are to be united and joined together when He said: 'Therefore they are no longer two, but one flesh'" (ibid., 20). In addition, in its description of marriage in a more general sense the encyclical builds on the notion of marriage as found in the Catechism of Trent. In the Catechism marriage is described as "a complete and intimate life partnership and association" (ibid., 24).

The documents that issued forth during the papacy of Pius XII repeatedly affirm that nature of marriage as a union. For example, in the *Address to the Midwives*, marriage as a union is described in the following:

> [I]n marriage the Creator has destined human beings, made of flesh and blood and endowed with a mind and a heart, for the procreation of new life, and they are called to be the parents of their progeny as human beings and not irrational animals. It is to this end that God wills the union of married people. Indeed Holy Writ says of God that he created human kind to his image, created them male and female, and willed—as we find repeatedly stated in the Holy Bible—that a man "shall leave father and mother, and shall cleave to his wife, and they shall be two in one flesh" (Pius XII 1951a [43], 845).

Further, the conjugal act is described as an action of persons which is characterized as the reciprocal gift of the spouses to each other which "according to the word of the Scriptures, effects the union 'in one flesh alone'" (ibid.). And again, the exercise of conjugal intercourse is characterized as the personal relation, as opposed to the biological relation to each other. This personal relation is the giving of themselves to each other (Pius XII 1956 [48], 470).

Gaudium et spes continues this affirmation of the essential nature of marriage as a union. The union is described in the traditional terms as developing as "a man and a woman, by their compact of conjugal love 'are no longer two, but one flesh' (Matt. 19:6)" (*Gaudium et spes* 48). The characterization of the union is enriched by notions, especially of the personal rather than bodily nature of the union, that began to emerge in the pontificate of Pius XII. *Gaudium et spes* describes marriage as an intimate union of actions and persons in which the "spouses mutually bestow and accept each other" (ibid.). The conjugal act is an immediate experience of oneness as each spouse gives and accepts each other in a "mutual gift of two persons" (ibid.).

Humanae vitae asserts the unitive nature of marriage in its description of marriage as an intimate community of love and life. It results from "the reciprocal personal gift" (Paul VI 1968, 8) of the spouses to each other. This reciprocal personal gift is characterized as a "communion of their being" (ibid.). The characterization of the gift as that of the person, rather than simply a gift of the body, is emphasized in the description of the formation of the marital union as "a way that, husband and wife become one heart and one soul" (ibid., 9).

In *Donum vitae*, the marital union is described in terms which suggest a personal communion of love. While union and procreation remain linked, nonetheless, the union is explicitly recognized. The instruction says. "God, who is love and life, has inscribed in man and woman the vocation to share in a special way his mystery of personal communion and in his work as Creator and Father" (*Donum vitae*, Intro., 3).

Contemporary Commentary

Contributions to the understanding of the meaning of marriage as an intimate personal union by love and in love have been made in the twentieth century. In the first half of the century, this interpretation was presented by those whose philosophical perspective earned for their works the designation Christian Personalism. Significant among those writers were Anton Koch, P. Fidelis Schwendinger, O.F.M., Dietrich von Hildebrand, and Herbert Doms. Their works, contemporaneous with *Casti connubii*, represent the distillation of thinking regarding the nature of marriage fermenting in this period. In describing the nature of marriage, Koch wrote,

> It is reasonable to suppose that the purpose of marriage is a sexual community ordained to quieten concupiscence and produce children. But the highest and principle purpose of marriage is undivided community of life between man and woman (Koch, *Lehrbuch der Moraltheologie*, in Doms 1939, xx).

And Father Schwendinger, writing in the influential theological review *Theologie und glaube*, described the essential nature of marriage in the following:

Unless we are prepared to maintain that the Church consecrates sacramentally an institution which has no meaning (i.e. an unfulfilled marriage like that of Joseph and Mary), we are bound to admit that marriage has some other meaning besides procreation and that this other meaning is essential to marriage. Community of personal life between husband and wife is the only possible other meaning. If we consider the psychological process which leads up to marriage ("falling in love," etc.), we must see that community of life is the first thing which the man and the woman desire. ... The *Me-You* community still remains the first thing when one looks at marriage objectively. The first thing that husband and wife want to do is not to create a third thing distinct from either. The third person is not that which unites them and makes them say *We*, nor do they fulfil and consummate each other through it. No, the first and most obvious characteristic of marriage is the direct union in love between a *Me* and a *You*. The object of their desire is *the whole person*. And when marriage is consummated each person gives and receives *an entire personality*. And this complete giving of the whole of a person to a person is for both human beings concerned the primary value and the meaning of marriage union (Schwendinger in Doms 1939, xx-xxi).

In the "Preface" to his essay on marriage, Hildebrand distinguishes between a primary end of marriage and a primary meaning of marriage. He continues, in line with the explicit statements within the tradition, to regard procreation as the primary end of marriage, but, in keeping with his personalist emphasis, he maintains that marriage also has a primary meaning which is "the intimate union of two persons in mutual love" (von Hildebrand 1942, v). In his description of the meaning of marriage as a personal union of love he says,

We have found that the primary meaning of marriage which enables it to serve as an image of the relationship between the soul and God, consists in that closest communion of love whereby two persons become one—one heart, one soul, one flesh (ibid., 33).

Hildebrand maintains that the marital union itself is an objective reality. He says,

> In the same way, the act of voluntary surrender of one's own person to another with the intention of forming a permanent and intimate union of love, creates an objective bond, which once established, is withdrawn from the sphere of arbitrary decision of the persons concerned. ... Both partners now belong wholly to each other, an objective bond unites them, they are no longer two but one (ibid., 18-19).

In his work, *The Meaning of Marriage*, Dr. Doms offers a description of the essential nature of marriage as an intimate personal relationship that forms a vital life in common, which he calls "der Zweieinigkeit." He describes this intrinsic meaning of marriage in the following:

> Marriage is legal, real and moral two-in-oneship. Marital love is its life breath. This love is of itself fruitful. Any experience of love puts people under the domination of that great law of love which embraces every human community and attains its supreme meaning in marriage. Indeed it then comes to play a determining part because of the completeness and intimacy of the community of life between married people (Doms 1939, 26).

Doms marshalls biological, psychological, and philosophical arguments to support his contention that "the immediate purpose of marriage is the realization of its meaning, the marital two-in-oneship" (ibid., 94).

During the papacy of Pope Pius XII, this understanding of marriage as an intimate personal union by love and in love was pushed into the background. However, it emerged from the shadows in the wake of Vatican II. It is found in the writings of contemporary commentators. The following is a representative sampling of such commentary. In *Catholic Sexual Ethics: A Summary, Explanation, & Defense*, Ronald Lawler, O.F.M. Cap., Joseph M. Boyle, Jr., and William E. May, develop the essential nature of marriage. They describe marriage as a procreative union and as a personal union forming a single subject through conjugal love of the spouses. The text says,

It is the union of one man and one woman, who mutually give themselves to each other so that they may share an intimate partnership of the whole of their lives until death. Their marital union, which is brought into being by their personal act of irrevocable consent, is of its own inner dynamism and nature ordered to the procreation and education of children and to the fostering of a special and exclusive kind of love—marital or spousal or conjugal love. As spouses, moreover, husband and wife form the single subject of a shared sexual life, and their marital union is fittingly expressed in and by an act proper and specific to them, the marital act. In this act they become "one flesh," and come to "know" one another in a unique and unforgettable way. Through it, spouses symbolize and support all the activities in which they share intimately their lives with each other and communicate the gift of life to new human persons (Lawler 1985, 135).

While Lawler, Boyle, and May affirm the personal union, they accord controlling status to marriage as a procreative union. Failure to take this understanding of marriage as a personal union into account and to give it controlling status results in the inability to defend such central notions of the tradition as monogamy as evidenced in a later work by Joseph Boyle. In his 1989 presidential address, "Marriage is an Institution Created by God: A Philosophical Analysis," to the American Catholic Philosophical Association, Boyle cannot defend monogamy in the presence of Alan Donagan's group procreative arrangement.

Karl Rahner in "Marriage As a Sacrament" raises the question as to what precisely is the core notion of marriage. He designates marriage as a sign and says of the sign,

It possesses this character prior to any theological consideration and prior to its bearing upon the relationship between Christ and the Church, because in itself it has a physical and social dimension of reality. Here we have the incarnation, as it were, the real symbol, the manifestation, the 'space-time' dimension, the most interior and most personal union in love of two individuals at the very roots of their being as oriented in freedom to God (Rahner 1973, 202).

Rahner says of this intimate and personal union between a man and a woman that it results in the formation of an intimate and exclusive relationship, a "'we', a relationship ... in which a 'we' is constituted which opens itself lovingly precisely to all" (ibid., 207).

Thomas A. Shannon and Lisa Sowle Cahill focus on marriage as an interpersonal relationship of persons in love in their work on the ethics of artificial reproduction. They offer this reflection in their assessment of the ambiguities in the Roman Catholic tradition on marriage in the following:

> [W]ithin the trinity of love, sex, and procreation, it is love that is fundamental, most humanly distinctive, and thus most morally important. Sex and procreation are not merely dispensable goods, but their moral meaning can be defined fully only within the interpersonal relationship of the persons who cooperate in realizing these goods (Shannon, 1988, 53).

Theodore Mackin in his explorations on marriage in the Roman Catholic tradition attempts a definition of marriage which he suggests must be a prescriptive definition of marriage. In the work "What Is Marriage?" which is directed to jurisprudential considerations, he says,

> I urge that the criterion and model for the prescriptive specifying element of the Catholic Church's definition of marriage be found in the sacrament. Note again that such criterion ought to contain the highest good, the ultimate goal that marriage as a societal relationship can bring to those who enter it, who create it by their mutual consent. Where men and women form this relationship as Christians, presumably they do so with the goal in mind that is the vision of God and his intimate love—do so with the intent to begin this vision and love this side of death in order to continue them endlessly beyond death.
>
> Presumably too they intend to make their way to the unending condition of this vision and love in the next life by experiencing in their marriages in this life a love that images the love of Christ and the Church. But this love was and is, before all else a self-giving and even sacrificial love—a self-donation made for the sake of the beloved's happiness.

This love has always been fertile, creative, constructive on the part of Christ in that it has bred in men and women in the Church belief, trust, selfless caring and the willingness to forgive and to heal damaged relationships. It has been fertile and creative on the Church's part in her striving in the persons of Christian men and women, to make up in their own lives what is still incomplete in the sufferings of Christ (Mackin 1982, 340-41).

The notion of marriage as an intimate personal union is found in the parenetic works, including the exhortation *Familiaris consortio*, of Pope John Paul II. In *Love and Responsibility*, he wrote, "in marriage two people, a man and a woman, are united in such a way that they become in a sense 'one flesh' (to use the words of the Book of Genesis), i.e., one common subject, as it were of sexual life" (Wojtyla 1981, 30). In *Familiaris consortio* he wrote,

> Conjugal love involves a totality, in which all the elements of the person enter—appeal of the body and instinct, power of feeling and affectivity, aspiration of the spirit and the will. It aims at a deeply personal unity, the unity that, beyond union in one flesh, leads to the forming of one heart and soul; it demands indissolubility and faithfulness in definitive mutual giving; and it is open to fertility (John Paul II 1981, 13).

While the Pontiff clearly intends here that the fertility be the fertility of children, further on in the same document he expands on the notion of fertility. He says in regard to the fecundity that is to mark married life that it "is enlarged and enriched by all those fruits of moral, spiritual, and supernatural life which father and mother are called on to hand on to their children and through the children to the church and to the world" (ibid., 28).

Marriage: A Specific Type of Human Relationship

The specific difference between this union and other types of human relationships are the following: (1) this relationship is the actual personal union of the partners, each of whom represents a partial manifestation of humanity to form a new being, the marriage; (2)

within this union, the procreation and education of children are to be accomplished; and (3) within this union, the flourishing of the individual partners, as individuals, is to be accomplished as each helps and satisfies the other. There are, then, three ends to be accomplished within marriage. They are the union itself, the children, and the flourishing of the individual partners. The subjects who constitute the marriage have specific identities as spouses, as parents, and as individuals.

Among the defining elements that are constitutive of the essential nature of marriage are that it is a covenanted, lifelong, heterosexual, sacramental union. Marriage is, by its nature ordered to the realization of the union, in which man and woman give and accept each other to establish a marriage. What distinguishes marriage as a community from other possible human communities such as brother/sister or a community of friends is the instantiation of the intimate personal union. This intimate personal union, which bears characteristics of both physical and moral unities, is a deeper union than either of these other types of union. It is a union of body, consciousness, and conscience. The union is a covenanted union. As a covenanted union, its love is marked by special elements. Among those elements are concern for the happiness of the beloved, concern for the fulfillment of the beloved, unfailing love, steadfast love, patience, and commitment. The covenanted love of God for Israel and the redeeming love of Christ for the Church serve as models for the marriage covenant. Because the covenant is difficult to sustain the grace of the sacrament is required. Within the matrix of the marital union the goods of the procreation and education of the children and the well being of the spouses are to be accomplished. Because these three ends, the generation of the union, the procreation and education of the children, and the perfection of the partners, require a long period of time to be accomplished, the indissolubility of the union is required. While the procreation and education of children would seem, in itself, to require longevity but not indissolubility in the marriage, the other ends, the continuation of the union and the perfection of the partners would seem to require indissolubility. The grace of the sacrament empowers the union and fortifies the indissolubility. Because the specifying determinants of the union that is marriage include the emergence of a personal union marked by ontological completeness, the procreation as well as the education of children, and the satisfaction of particular desires, the union is heterosexual. Because the marriage, the partners, and the children all have a transcendental end, the grace of the sacrament is required to accomplish the good which is beyond nature. This understanding of the essential nature of marriage has been made explicit in the present *Code of Canon Law*. Canon 1055 states in its first section:

> The marriage covenant, by which a man and a woman establish between themselves a partnership of their whole life, and which of its own very nature is ordered to the well-being of the spouses and to the procreation and upbringing of children, has, between the baptized, been raised by Christ the Lord to the dignity of a sacrament (*Code of Canon Law* 1983, Canon 1055, 1).

Ends of Marital Union

Three ends, then, are to be accomplished in marriage. They are the personal union itself, the children, and the flourishing of the individual persons. These ends may be differentiated as intrinsic-necessary and intrinsic-contingent. The designation intrinsic denotes accomplishment within the union. The further differentiation as intrinsic-necessary and intrinsic-contingent derives from the fact that some ends are always accomplished, while others are accomplished, if accomplished at all, with statistical regularity. The union is the intrinsic-necessary end. Marriage is always a union. The conjugal act is always unitive. The realization of offspring is an intrinsic-contingent end. As intrinsic, it is to be accomplished within marriage. Marriage supplies the matrix of conditions for children. As contingent, it is to be accomplished only sometimes within the marriage. The conjugal act is appropriately exercised within marriage and is sometimes reproductive. The contingent character of reproduction within marriage is a matter of biological fact. The contingent character of reproduction within the exercise of the conjugal act is a matter of psychological fact. It is also a matter of consistent teaching within the tradition. The marriage of Mary and Joseph remains a marriage even though there are no offspring of the marriage. The tradition recognizes the continuation of the marriage even in the presence of the loss of procreative power of either partner. The marriage of the permanently sterile and the marriage of the elderly is sanctioned within the tradition even though the possibility of children is excluded from these marriages. The distinction between *potentia coeundi* and *potentia generandi* (Pius XII 1954 [45], 676) with the recognition that the former is a necessary requirement for a valid marriage while the latter is not, contributes to the assessment that marriage is, in its essential nature a union between a man and a woman that is sometimes procreative. The realization of the personalist-individual ends, including the satisfaction of the sexual appetite, is an intrinsic-contingent end. As intrinsic, it is to be accomplished within the marriage. Marriage supplies the matrix of conditions for the realization of these ends. As contingent these ends, remediation of concupiscence and mutual aid, are sometimes accomplished in marriage and are sometimes accomplished by one or the other partner while at the same time it is given by the other partner as "rendering the debt." The ordination of the marriage act itself is to serve in the accomplishment of these specific ends. The conjugal act is appropriately exercised within marriage in the service of these ends. A similar differentiation in the character of the ends of marriage is also found in the earlier teachings of the tradition. In the work of Alphonsus Liguori, the ends of marriage are distinguished as intrinsic or extrinsic and essential or accidental. The classification of ends by Ligouri from within these categories is as follows:

> (1) intrinsic and essential, (2) intrinsic and accidental; and (3) extrinsic and accidental. There are two ends of the first kind: "the mutual giving with the obligation of returning the debt, and the indissoluble bond." Both the indissolubility and the giving of the right to one's body for intercourse were intrinsic ends of marriage. The ends of the second category were the procreation of offspring and the remedying of concupiscence. The ends of the third category were several: "to conciliate feuds, to obtain pleasure, and so forth." (*Moral Theology* 6.882) (Noonan 1986, 328).

If the differentiation of ends as intrinsic-necessary and intrinsic-contingent correctly describes the several ends to be accomplished within marriage, then the claim that there is an inseparable nexus between the procreative meaning and the unitive meaning in every act of conjugal intercourse can no longer be maintained. From this understanding of marriage as essentially a personal union, a union that is to serves as the matrix of conditions for specific procreative and personalist ends, follows a new understanding of the inseparable connection between the unitive and procreative significance. The inseparable connection between the unitive and procreative cannot be maintained, as a natural law claim, that is an order discernible in the nature of marriage and its acts, if by inseparable connection is meant that every act of conjugal intercourse must signify both. Both physically and psychologically they are separate as ends of the act of intercourse. The inseparable connection between the unitive and procreative can be maintained, if what is meant is that sexual intercourse is inseparable from the marital union. It is appropriate only within marriage. And within marriage, intercourse serves the goods of the marriage.

Sets of Ends within the Marital Union

Within the matrix of this personal union that is marriage, the several distinct ends, namely, the unitive which intends the partnership—the sacred bond, the procreative which intends the children, and the personalist which intends the well-being of the spouses, press for actualization on three distinct but interrelated levels. The unitive end, in which there is an ontological transformation of the individuals into spouses, is directed to the flourishing of the union—the new personal organism that is brought into being with the marriage. The procreative finality in which there is an ontological transformation of the individual partners into parents is directed to the procreation and education of children. The personalist end is directed to the flourishing of the individuals, as individuals, who form the union. The accomplishment of each of these ends is marked by sets of interrelated levels of finality, namely, horizontal, vertical, and transcendental. The examination of the emerging position on marriage will proceed with (1) the explicitation of the levels of finality, (2) the specific delineation of the ends of marriage from within the framework of the levels of finality, and (3) the examination of the consequences of the position developed within this framework on the accomplishment or avoidance of the reproductive finality.

Levels of Finality

Finality, or final causality, is the operation of causation as directed to an end as good, that is, as perfective of the being. The notion of final causality, which entered philosophy with Aristotle, has been described by Bernard Lonergan in the following: "[T]here is final causality if, and only if, appetite responds because the motive is good; if and only if, process is oriented because the term is good" (Lonergan 1967b, 19). The types of final causality along with their respective ends are as follows:

FINALITY		END
a) horizontal	—>	essential good
b) vertical	—>	excellent good
c) transcendental	—>	absolute good

The level of horizontal finality is the reference of each thing to its commensurate motives and ends. It is abstract essence that determines horizontal finality. Lonergan describes the determination by essence of horizontal finality in the following:

> [T]he ground of such limitation is essence: remotely it is substantial essence; proximately it is the essence of the ontological accident, the essence, say, of sensitive appetite, of rational appetite, of infused charity; for it is essence that limits, that ties things down to a given type, that assign them their proper and proportionate ends (ibid., 19).

Because of its determination by essence, the accomplishment of an end on the horizontal level is designated as the essential good. Lonergan says of horizontal finality, "it holds even when the object is in isolation; it is a motive or term that is proportionate to essence" (ibid., 21).

Vertical finality directs to attainment at a higher level of activity. Vertical finality is the upward dispositive thrust which propels process and appetite from lower to higher levels. Its accomplishment requires the complementarity of the concrete plurality. Lonergan describes four types of vertical finality. They are instrumental, dispositive, material, and obediential. Instrumental finality is described as causal action in which, "a concrete plurality of lower activities may be instrumental to a higher end in another subject: the many movements of the chisel give beauty to the statue" (ibid., 19). Dispositive finality is described as an upthrust within a subject or within an organism, for example, "the many sensitive experiences of research lead to the act of understanding that is scientific inquiry" (ibid., 20). Material finality describes causal action in which, "a concrete plurality of lower entities may be the material cause from which a higher form is educed or into which a subsistent form is infused" (ibid.). The union of gametes to form a zygote or of hydrogen and oxygen to form water are instances of material finality. Obediential finality requires the disposition of the subject and is realized in the operation of "a concrete plurality of rational beings ... to receive the communication of God ... its principal unfolding in the habitation of the Holy Spirit by sanctifying grace, and its ultimate consummation in the beatific vision" (ibid., 21). Because vertical finality directs to the attainment at a higher level of activity than horizontal finality, its accomplishment is designated as the excellent good. Lonergan describes vertical finality in the following:

> Vertical finality is in the concrete; in point of fact it is not from the isolated instance but from the conjoined plurality; it is in the field not of natural but of statistical law, not of the abstract *per se* but of the concrete *per accidens* (ibid.).

On the level of transcendental finality, the reference of all things is to God. In regard to transcendental finality, Thomas Aquinas says, "all things, desire God" (Aquinas, *De veritate*, q. 22, a. 2), and again, "all things intend to be assimilated to God" (Aquinas, *Summa contra gentiles* III, ch. 19, 1). Lonergan describes transcendental finality as the response in a hierarchical universe of limited beings that each on its level of reality "responds to God as absolute motive and tends to him as absolute term ..." (Lonergan 1967b, 19). The attainment of the end on the transcendental level is the attainment of the absolute good. Hence, its accomplishment is more excellent than that on the level of vertical finality. There are, then, three distinct levels of finality and three distinct goods, namely, the essential, the excellent, and the absolute good. Each lower level has a dispositive function. Actualization on the lower level is propadeutic to the emergence of activity on the higher level. Each higher level has a transforming function. It qualitatively alters the activity on the lower level. In describing the interrelated activities of these levels of finality Lonergan says,

> Finally, these three levels are realized in one subject; as the higher perfects the lower, so the lower disposes to the higher; and it is in this disposition of natural spontaneity to reinforce reason, of reason to reinforce grace—for all three come from and return to God (ibid., 29).

Ends of Marriage As Levels of Finality

The examination of the ends of marriage from within the framework of the levels of finality follows. The union is the intrinsic necessary end of marriage. The act of conjugal intercourse is the act which signifies and instantiates the union. The realization of the union on various levels of finality with their respective ends is as follows:

Finality	End	Specific End
a) horizontal	essential good	organistic union
b) vertical	excellent good	union of friendship
c) transcendental	absolute good	union with God

On the level of horizontal finality, the union emerges as a consequence of a basic form of appetition in which human beings as male and female are properly attracted to and properly respond to one another. This pleasurable experience acts upon the relationship in such as way that the relationship is more easily disposed to the transforming power of reason. Both Aristotle and Thomas Aquinas comment on this. On the level of vertical finality the transforming power of reason operates within the organistic union and brings about the emergence of friendship between the spouses. This integration of reason and intense passion, as habitual and reciprocal, forms the set of conditions which incline toward the emergence of unity of consciousness and unity of conscience. This triple unity of body, consciousness, and conscience supplies the fertile matrix for the sustained development of the spouses that makes the marital union receptive to the transforming power of grace. It is only with the elevating power of grace that the spouses are brought to the possibility of attainment of the absolute good which is God. This ascent from passion to friendship to total love within marriage has been described by Bernard Lonergan. Lonergan says,

> Not only is it true that man should love other objects in virtue of his love of God; it is also true that he can love God only in an ascent through participated to absolute excellence. Thus love of others is proof of love of God: "God himself dwells in us if we love one another; his love is brought to perfection within us" (John 4: 12) ... Now toward this high goal of charity it is no small beginning in the weak and imperfect heart of fallen man to be startled by a beauty that shifts the center of appetition out of self; and such a shift is effected on the level of sensitive spontaneity by *eros* leaping in through delighted eyes and establishing itself as unrest in absence and an imperious demand for company. Next company may reveal deeper qualities of mind and character to shift again the center from the merely organistic tendencies of nature to the rational friendship with its enduring basis in the excellence of the good person. Finally grace inserts into charity the love that nature gives and reason approves. Thus we have a dispositive upward tendency from *eros* to friendship, and from friendship to a special order of charity (ibid., 31).

The correlative movement, the transforming power of the highest level on the lower level, is described by Dietrich von Hildebrand in his essay on marriage. He says,

> *Conjugal love* undergoes a deep, even a *qualitative* change in the living members of the Mystical Body of Christ. Not that wedded love ceases to have the characteristics discussed above: mutual self-giving, the character of an *I-thou* communion, the living for each other, and the formation of a complete unity as a couple closed off

from the rest of earthly things. Indeed it does not cease in any way
to be conjugal love in the full sense of the word. The supernatural
does not dissolve this finest earthly good, but transfigures it (von
Hildebrand 1942, 34).

The procreative ends are the intrinsic-contingent ends of marriage.
As intrinsic they are to be accomplished within marriage. As contingent
they are to be accomplished occasionally within marriage. The contingent nature of the procreative end derives from the biological fact that
procreation is accomplished only occasionally in conjugal intercourse
and from the prudential judgment that reasonable and responsible
parenthood is accomplished only when children are brought into existence in the appropriate circumstances and for the proper motives.
The realization of the procreative ends on various levels of finality
with their respective ends is as follows:

Finality	End	Specific End
a) horizontal	essential good	existence
b) vertical	excellent good	education
c) transcendental	absolute good	union with God

On the horizontal level, the procreative end is accomplished in the
emergence in existence of the new human being. The new human being
most likely emerges with the completion of the process of syngamy,
that is, with the fusion of the chromosomal materials of the maternal
and paternal pronuclei. The act of conjugal intercourse accomplishes
insemination not fertilization. In the act of conjugal intercourse, the
male germ cell is placed in proximity to the female germ cell. That is,
it is placed in the same physical system as the ovum. In time, which
may vary from a few hours to a few days, the male germ cell may
reach the site of the female germ cell. If the sperm arrives at the distal
end of the fallopian tubes at the time when a mature ovum is present, the capacitated sperm may penetrate the zona pellucida of the
ovum and fertilization may occur. Procreation is distant in time and
place from the act of conjugal intercourse. Furthermore, the relation
of intercourse to procreation is a matter of statistical frequency not a
matter of necessary connection. Even in those instances in which the

anatomy is appropriate, the incidence of reproduction is measured in terms of probability.

The vertical finality in regard to the procreative end of marriage is accomplished in the education of children. Through education and moral training, the faculties of children are developed so that they may share in the goods of human life. The transcendental finality, which is reached only in union with God, is served within the marriage as parents contribute to the interior formation of their children in such a way as to dispose them to the movement of grace. While the accomplishment of the vertical and transcendental finalities of the procreative end of marriage requires prior actualization of the horizontal finality, accomplishment of the horizontal finality is reasonable and responsible only in those circumstances in which the accomplishment of the vertical and the transcendental finality is a real possibility.

The personalist ends are also intrinsic-contingent ends of marriage. They are those individual ends which are to be accomplished by the partners of the marriage inasmuch as the partners maintain their individuality despite their ontological transformation into spouses and parents. The realization of the personalist goods on the various levels of finality with their respective ends is as follows:

Finality	End	Specific End
a) horizontal	essential good	maintenance of life
b) vertical	excellent good	good life
c) transcendental	absolute good	life of grace

In regard to the personalist end, achievement on the horizontal level is the accomplishment of the maintenance of life. This is the level of sensitive appetite and this appetite as inclination is the "inclination to good in accordance with the nature which is had in common with all substances ... seeking the preservation of its own being ... and whatever is a means of preserving human life and warding off its obstacles ..." (Aquinas, *Summa theologiae* I-II, q. 94, a. 2). This is the essential good that is the requisite condition for the accomplishment of all other goods. The sharing of work within marriage inclines toward the enhancement of the good of life. On the vertical level where there is the upthrust from lower to higher levels of appetition, the end to be accomplished is the more excellent end, that of the good life. While the essential good of life is required for the accomplishment of the higher end, the good life, it is not sufficient of itself. Vertical finality requires the complementarity of the concrete plurality to accomplish its ends. One can accomplish the good life, an observation at least as old as the *Nicomachean Ethics* of Aristotle, only in the presence and with the cooperation of others.

Many attempts have been made throughout the history of philosophy to list the elements of the good life. Among the earliest and most systematic is that delineated by Aristotle in the *Nicomachean Ethics*. Aristotle's list includes speculative and practical knowledge, temperance, courage, justice, friendship, moderation and magnificence in the use of money, honor, gentleness, appropriate intercourse of language. Another list can be culled from the writings of Saint Thomas Aquinas. That list as developed and classified according to categories of contemporary sociology includes health, wealth, knowledge, beauty, sociability, and religion (Smith 1915, 55). Health includes individual integrity, work and sex. Wealth includes mastery over things and as well as accumulation of things. Knowledge is both speculative and practical. Sociability includes recognition and reciprocal valuation. A contemporary list from the domain of philosophy is presented by John Finnis who lists the basic forms of human good as the following: life as vitality, knowledge, play, aesthetic knowledge, sociability, practical reasonableness, and "religion" (Finnis 1980, 85ff). A contemporary list from the domain of psychology is presented by Abraham Maslow who groups the human goods into five distinct categories of needs. They are physiological needs, safety needs, acceptance needs, esteem needs, and the need for self actualization. They are arranged in hierarchical order from the lowest level of physiological needs to the highest level of self-actualization needs. The accomplishment of the higher levels requires prior accomplishment of the lower level (Barone 1989, 379). The conjugal union is the foundational institution for the possibility of the good life.

On the transcendental level, which is the reference of all things to God, the supernatural end of man begins as response to God as motive and ends when union with God as absolute term is achieved. The accomplishment of this most excellent end requires the transforming power of grace. Marriage as a total life in common provides the conditions that nurture the pursuit of human and eternal goods. Lonergan says,

> [M]arriage ... has as its primary reason and cause a mutual influence, a sustained effort of common improvement, tending to the very summit of Christian perfection. Any insertion of spontaneous union or human friendship into charity, which is friendship in Christ, has not the ground of supernatural excellence achieved but the end of such excellence to be achieved. It follows that the compenetrating consciousness of lives shared by marriage is dynamic and reaches forth to will and to realize in common the advance in Christian perfection that leads from the consummation of two-in-one-flesh to the consummation of the beatific vision (Lonergan 1967, 37).

While the vertical good is more excellent in reference to the horizontal good, it is less excellent in reference to the transcendental good.

In summary, marriage, in its essential nature, is an intimate personal union. This intimate personal union supplies the matrix of conditions in which children may flourish and the partners of the marriage may flourish. In marriage there are three distinct sets of ends to be accomplished on interrelated levels. The distinct ends are the union, children, and individual human goods. The union is the intrinsic necessary end of the marriage. The good of children and the good of the partners are the intrinsic contingent ends of marriage. The levels of finality are horizontal, vertical, and transcendental. The horizontal is primary in the sense that it is a first level of actualization. Furthermore, its actualization serves as a congenial foundation for the emergence of the higher level. The vertical raises the horizontal to the level of human activity and it is dispositive for the reception of the activity that mediates the process to the level of transcendental finality. As an intimate personal union, marriage has similarities to a physical unity and similarities to a moral unity. However, it is neither. It is a unique kind of union. As a personal union it is closer, deeper, and more intense than a physical union. As a personal union, it goals and range of activities, encompassing all human activities, is more comprehensive than the goals and set of activities of any other moral union. In its similarity to a physical unity, the marriage is a unity subsisting in itself. It is a unity on the level of essence. The spouses, as spouses, are related to the whole, which is the marital union, as integral part to whole. The spouses, precisely as spouses, are destined in their very being to be inserted into the whole which is the marriage. In its similarity to a moral unity, the marriage is a unity on the level of action. The common action to achieve both the goals of the family and the individual goals of the members of the family draws the family into a unity. In the accomplishment of its ends on the level of horizontal finality, it most closely resembles a physical unity. For example, in the accomplishment of reproduction as a horizontal finality, the complementary organs of reproduction of the spouses form a single physical system which tends toward the emergence of a new individual. In the accomplishment of its ends as vertical and transcendental finalities, it more closely resembles a moral unity. In those instances in which the marriage resembles a physical unity, the governance of action is accomplished by application of the principle of totality as it applies to other physical unities.

Conjugal intercourse is the marriage act. As expressive of the reality of marriage it must always signify the marital union. Conjugal intercourse is appropriate within marriage to nourish the marital union. Conjugal intercourse is appropriate within marriage to realize the end which is the good of children. The good of children may be sought in marriage under the conditions of reasonableness and responsibility. Furthermore, conjugal intercourse is appropriate within marriage to satisfy the individual needs of the partners. While the particular need may be experienced as an exigency by one partner and the rendering of the debt by the other partner, the satisfaction of the need contributes to the good of the partner and serves the good of the marriage union. These individual goods may be sought in marriage under the governance of chastity and friendship.

In its objective determination, conjugal intercourse is an act which is always unitive, sometimes procreative, and sometimes personalist. Conjugal intercourse most completely signifies the reality that is marriage when it realizes in a single act all the distinct ends of marriage. However, that realization is not possible, as a matter of fact, and is not appropriate, as a matter of prudential judgment, in every act of conjugal intercourse. The accomplishment of all the ends, as far as possible, on the interrelated levels of finality is the function of the marriage vocation, that is, they are to be accomplished over time.

The Emerging Notion: Marriage As a Union

Consequences for Reproductive Finality

Having completed a more precise profile of the nature of marriage, and having made more explicit the sets of ends of marriage, the next task is the consideration of the consequences of this more complete account on the governance of the reproductive finality. The controlling notions that are to direct the reproductive finality, whether the intention be accomplishment or avoidance, are as follows:

1. The marital union, in itself, is the relevant ethical entity. Marriage is an intimate personal union that bears similarities to a physical union and similarities to a moral union.

2. Reproduction is to be accomplished within the vocation of marriage.

3. Accomplishment of reproduction requires the prior existence of conditions within the marriage which are conducive to the possibility of the emergence of higher levels of existence for the child.

4. In respect to reproduction as a horizontal finality, the marital partners are integral parts of the totality that is the physical union, which if, anatomically intact and chemically correct, tends to the accomplishment of reproduction.

5. The principles that apply to other physical unities are to be applied to the avoidance or accomplishment of the reproductive finality on the level of horizontal finality.

The judgment that the circumstances of a particular marriage require that reproduction be avoided, is to be the prudential judgment of the marriage partners. The accomplishment of the intrinsic-contingent end of children as a horizontal finality is contrary to reasonable and responsible parenthood unless there exists the conditions for the possibility of the emergence for the child of the higher levels of finality. Reasonable means may be utilized, for a determinate or an indeterminate time, to prevent procreation within particular acts of conjugal intercourse within the vocation of marriage. These means include rhythm, contraception, and sterilization. The choice of means should be a function of the seriousness of the reasons for the avoidance of procreation. The more serious the problem, the more certain should be the manner of reproduction limitation. In very serious circumstances, that is, where pregnancy threatens the life or health of the spouse and hence represents a real threat to the very existence of the marital union as a personal union, sterilization of either member, as an application of the principle of totality, is appropriate.

The judgment that the circumstances of a particular marriage require that artificial means, including homologous artificial insemination or homologous in vitro fertilization and embryo transfer, be utilized in order that reproduction be accomplished is to be the prudential judgment of the marriage partners. In the presence of defects in the physical system that serves to accomplish the reproductive end on the level of horizontal finality and in the presence of conditions in the marriage that are conducive to the emergence for the offspring of the higher levels of finality, reasonable means may be used to accomplish procreation. The choice of means should be a function of the specific physical defect to be remedied. Because procreation in its natural occurrence is distant in time and place from the act of insemination, the accomplishment of reproduction by artificial means may be distant in time and place from the act of conjugal intercourse.

Chapter 4

Epilogue:
Response to the Questions

It has been almost ten years now since the first edition of *Finality and Marriage* appeared in print. In that time, many questions have been raised about the ideas presented therein and many comments have been received about the text. Most of the comments have been favorable. They assess the work as a contribution which advances the Catholic teaching on marriage and the goods to be accomplished within marriage. These comments have come from a variety of sources, married couples, single people, religious men and women, philosophers, theologians, and just plain folks. The most frequently occurring comment has been, "It just makes sense."

Some of the comments and questions, however, have not been so favorable. The latter fall into the following categories: (A) the work is incorrect and it represents a departure from the Catholic teaching on marriage; (B) the work is correct as far as it goes but incomplete, that is, it does not address the possibility of same sex marriage; and (C) the work is correct but incomplete, that is, it fails to apply the theoretical in any practical way that is useful for married couples. Each one of these will be considered separately, but briefly.

Incorrect because Different

A Departure from Catholic Tradition on Marriage

The assessment that *Finality and Marriage* is incorrect because it is a departure from the teaching of the tradition is usually embedded in the related set of claims (1) that the teachings of the Church do not change, (2) that the traditional teaching has a natural law foundation and the nature of marriage does not change, (3) that any admission of the possibility of change is an attack on the very integrity of the teaching function of the Church, (4) that the position developed is proportionalist and proportionalism is an inadequate ethical theory.

1. Development of Teachings of the Church

While there is great stability in Catholic teaching, the teachings of the Church have changed over time. This should present a problem for no one who has studied the history of the Church. Change in teaching has, as a matter of historical fact, occurred in both the speculative and practical domains of theology. On the speculative side, attempts to express and to find appropriate language to express the mystery of the Trinity and to express the dignity of Mary serve as two of the clearest examples. Early attempts to give an account, using material symbols, of the Trinity failed. The account of the Trinity proffered by Augustine, based on the understanding of the operations of the mind and the procession of the interior words, was more satisfying. The Augustinian account, while not dispelling the mystery, afforded the mind some repose. The understanding of the role of Mary has advanced as her role as the Mother of God, her Immaculate Conception, and her Assumption have been proclaimed.

On the practical side of theological development, there is an extensive list of changes including the transition: (a) from the acceptance of slavery to its condemnation, (b) from the prohibition of usury to the acceptance of capitalist, but not materialist, principle of the right of the individual to use money to make money, (c) from the indissolubility of marriage to the dissolution of certain marriages for the sake of faith, and (d) from the requirement of the persecution of heretics and from the teaching that "outside the Church there is no salvation," to the declaration of religious freedom (Noonan 1993, 662-69). A most recent change is present in the transition from the acceptance of capital punishment as an appropriate societal means of self-defense to the reluctant acceptability of capital punishment in only the rarest of circumstances, that is, "very rare, if in fact they [the circumstances] occur at all" (*Evangelium vitae*, 1995, 56).

How are these changes to be understood? That is, how can it be maintained that, at one and the same time, the Church is the repository of truth and that there is development of doctrine? That these changes represent development in doctrine cannot be denied. However, the advance in teaching is not a change in truth but a change in understanding of the truth, that is, "Insight grows both into the words and the realities that have been handed on" (Vatican II, *Dei verbum* 8, Second Vatican Council, *Constitutiones* 430). The human intellect in its relentless press for understanding and in its ongoing normative operations supplies the dynamism and the direction of the development of understanding. The resultant new insight is sometimes the type of change that is development and sometimes the type of change that is correction. Changes in the understanding of usury, slavery, marriage, capital punishment, and religious freedom have come about as the core principles regarding their understanding have been replaced by other principles. John T. Noonan describes the change this way.

> These principles were replaced by principles already part of Christian teaching: in the case of usury, that the person of the lender, not the loan, should be the focus of evaluation; in the case of marriage, that the preservation of faith is more important than preservation of a human relationship; in the case of slavery, that in Christ there is "neither free nor slave" (Gal. 3:28); and in the case of religious liberty, that faith must be free. In the course of this displacement of one set of principles, what was forbidden became lawful (the cases of usury and marriage); what was permissible became unlawful (the case of slavery); and what was required became forbidden (the persecution of heretics) (Noonan 1993, 669).

Similarly, John Henry Newman in his *Essay on Development of Doctrine* describes the developmental change not as a matter of deduction but as the result of the hard work of men and women utilizing the powers of the mind to approach a better understanding of the truth. Newman says,

> The development then of an idea is not like an investigation worked out on paper, in which each successive advance is pure evolution from a foregoing, but it is carried on through and by means of

communities of men and their leaders and guides; and it employs their minds as its instruments and depends upon them while it uses them. . . . It is the warfare of ideas under their varying aspects striving for the mastery. . . . (John Henry Newman, *Essay on Development of Doctrine* 1.1.6, p. 74.).

The expanded teaching on marriage that is presented here is a development from principles already part of Christian teaching, namely that marriage is a union. In its development, focus shifts from the organs of the spouses and from the man and woman as individuals to the marriage union itself. It is an effort to respond to the renewal, which eschews theological positivism, called forth by Vatican II that demanded that moral theology not only be nourished by Scripture and be linked to dogma but also be scientifically and philosophically grounded (Servais Pinckaers, O.P., *The Splendor of Christian Life*, pp 4-5).

2. The Nature of Marriage:

The natural law foundation reaffirmed

Natural law thinkers in the Thomist tradition tend to hold that the proximate source of natural law precepts is the activity of the human reason (*recta ratio*) as it apprehends human nature (*natura*) and the goods as ends, not wants or desires, of human flourishing and commands that those goods be fulfilled. Disagreements among contemporary natural law thinkers in the Thomist tradition have their source in their varying emphases on *natura* and *recta ratio*. All those in this tradition affirm that the nature of marriage does not change. Marriage is not a social construct. Marriage is a reality in the objective order. Marriage has an essential nature as a particular type of human relationship, that is, an intimate personal union of one man and one woman. Over time the essential nature of marriage has been explicated. Just as the understanding of other objective realities including those in the material world changes over time, so too has the understanding of marriage. To take an example from the material world, the periodic chart used in chemistry contains the list of all the known elements and their properties. It did not always look as it does today and a hundred years from now, perhaps, it will be more complete or have an entirely different appearance as chemistry is reduced to physics. The elements of the material world do not change, but attempts at understanding the elements and delineating their nature are more or less successful as the mind is more or less attentive, intelligent, understanding, and responsible and as collaborative contributions are made by the related sciences.

Similarly, the understanding and, hence, the teaching on the nature of marriage has developed in the history of the Church.

The discernment of the nature of marriage continued in the twentieth century and will continue through the twenty-first. In this expansion, marriage is affirmed as an objective reality, however the understanding of this reality develops as men and women of both faith and expertise attempt to fathom this great mystery and to enunciate its truth. The change may be described in broad stokes from the fifth century to the present. Augustine, writing in fifth century, listed three ends of marriage, namely, *proles, fides*, and *sacramentum*. In the latter part of the twentieth century, official Vatican documents list two inseparable ends of marriage, procreation and union. So the stated ends move from three to two and the two ends are said to be related in a particular way, that is, as inseparable from each other in every marriage act . The language of inseparability is new. It appeared for the first time in the writings of Pope Pius XII where he developed the notion in response to the challenge of artificial insemination. It was the claim of Pius XII that procreation is inseparable from the marriage of the two people who constitute a particular marital union. "The child," the Holy Father says, "is the fruit of the conjugal union when that union finds full expression by bringing into play the organic functions, the associated sensible emotions, and the spirited and disinterested love which animates the union" (Pius XII 1954 [48], 470). It is within the marital union "in one flesh alone" that procreation is to be accomplished. Artificial insemination violates the unitive, personalist, relational aspects of marriage. This emphasis on union as controlling is in itself a development for which Doms and others prepared the shift in direction.

The enunciation of the inseparability principle, that is that procreation and union are inseparable aspects of each and every act of conjugal intercourse, in *Humanae vitae* is a new development. The Holy Father, Paul VI, acknowledges that the, "new state of things gives rise to new questions," (Paul VI 1968, 3) and he calls for men and women of good faith and expertise to apply their wisdom to the issues in the encyclical. And as men and women of good faith respond to the request of the Holy Father, the teaching will develop. What is essential to marriage will be reaffirmed and what is inessential and/or the product of individual or group bias will be discarded. However, there is no guarantee of uninterrupted progress, as Lonergan reminded us, "while there is progress and while its principle is liberty, there is also decline and its principle is bias . . . to ignore the fact of decline was the error of the old liberal views of automatic progress" (Lonergan 1964, p. 260).

In *Humanae vitae*, Paul VI acknowledged the incredible progression of humankind in the extension of dominion and rational control over all aspects of life. He recognized that this rational control as subject to a loving God has limits and has as its goal the good life for human beings, that is, human flourishing. The gift of being in the world as men and women and the gift of marriage set limits and ends for human flourishing. However, it is not just marriage, but the good marriage that is the end as goal of men and women who are partners in the vocation of marriage. It is not just the existence of children, but their flourishing as rational beings and as God's children destined to union with God that is the struggle of men and women who are parents in the vocation of marriage. It is not just exquisite sensual pleasure, but that pleasure as it disposes toward the progression to friendship and then to love that is the promise realized by men and women who share the joy of the vocation of marriage. It is this notion of the *bene esse* of marriage that Rev. Richard A. McCormick explored in his final paper presented to the Catholic Theological Society of America in the Spring of 1999.

There are a variety of reasons for the ongoing development in the understanding of marriage. Some of the ideas have their source in the development of the sciences, both the hard and soft sciences, that is biology, psychology, and sociology, and the impact of that new knowledge on the understanding of marriage. It is important to recall that the scientific understanding of conception as the process of fertilization of the ovum by the sperm in the distal end of the Fallopian tube was, as a scientific accomplishment, a rather recent event, that is, it required the development of technology that became available only at the end of the nineteenth century. Understanding continued to develop in the twentieth century as for example the necessity of the sperm for capacitation. Similarly, the interaction of physical and psychological events, that is, such studies as the effects of the hormones, and the level of hormones, on the emotive responses of persons to each other and the development of friendships, including the friendship of marriage is a development of the Twentieth Century. Citing the development in the understanding of the nature of physical and chemical and social events is not to be viewed as an instance of the naturalistic fallacy. Rather it should be seen as the development of the Aristotelian-Thomist notion that there are potentialities within human beings both as individual and as related. The fulfillment of these potentialities is perfective of the human and, hence, ought to be realized. They, the potentialities, ought to be actualized. Knowledge of both the potentialities and of the conditions that facilitate their accomplishment is beneficial to the flourishing of the person.

3. The Integrity of the Teaching Function of the Church

Attacks on the integrity of the teaching function of the church are not new in the long history of the Church. In her teaching function, the Church, through the agency of her human members, is subject to all the vicissitudes and barriers that affect human beings in the pursuit of truth. There is risk to the integrity of the teaching role from a variety of sources including persistent theological positivism and its refusal to weigh and marshal evidence that might facilitate the emergence of new insights as well as the post modern full court press to deny the possibility of the objectivity of knowledge and the real nature of objects of knowledge. The first is the error of fundamentalism; the second is the error of skepticism. Both simply appear in their contemporary attire respectively dowdy or gauzy. The integrity of the teaching authority is guarded by remaining open to all the relevant questions and remaining prudential in pronouncement until sufficient evidence is present for that kind judgment, judgment as virtually unconditioned, within the grasp of the intellect. Need one be reminded of the present response to Galileo and Luther?

4. The Question of Proportionalism

The position that has been presented on the nature of marriage in this text is not a proportionalist position if what is meant by a proportionalism is a theory that denies the possibility of objective moral absolutes and a theory that regards human choice in its most critical moments as the choice of the lesser evil. An appropriately adequate account of the complexity of human existence and human striving requires due attention to both the proportionalist claims and the absolutist claims. The former pay insufficient attention to *natura* and the latter pay insufficient attention to the role of *recta ratio* in the judgment of practical reason that is central to moral life. In opposition to the proportionalist, the claim is made that marriage has a nature as an intimate personal union between a man and a woman for a lifetime and that certain goods are to be accomplished in marriage. The goods of marriage are differentiated as intrinsic necessary and intrinsic contingent. To directly intend the frustration of the accomplishment of those ends when the circumstances of the marriage are appropriate for their realization is to choose to violate the objective ordination of marriage. In opposition to the absolutist, the claim in regard to the nature of marriage and its goods is the same. To directly intend the accomplishment of those ends when the circumstances of the marriage are inappropriate for their realization is to choose to violate the rational ordination of marriage. In the assessment of the morality of an act, all three components—object, circumstances, and intention must be assessed. The specification of the object of the moral act as marriage understood as an intimate personal union with intrinsic necessary and intrinsic contingent ends capable of realization on various levels requires careful attendance to the circumstances of the particular marriage in the accomplishment of those ends which are intrinsic contingent.

Incorrect because Incomplete

Possibility of Homosexual Marriage

Does the specification of the nature of marriage as an intimate personal union lead to the possibility of same sex marriage? Any attempt to discuss the possibility of homosexual unions or to discuss the nature of homosexuality is to tread on ground that is both explosive and murky. The explosive nature of the discussion lies in the fact that anyone, whether the most disinterested scientist or the most compassionate pastor, who would raise the question of the nature of homosexuality risks being labeled "homophobic." The murkiness of the discussion lies in the fact that the study of the nature of homosexuality, as well as its etiology whether material or situational, is itself in inchoate form. Nonetheless, the task of the philosopher remains the pursuit of wisdom, despite the possibility of being labeled "homophobic" or "corrupter of youth" and despite the unpopularity of the study. So the question must be addressed, claims must be presented and defended, and counterclaims must be examined and, where possible, reversed. The philosopher has not the luxury of remaining on the sidelines. The response to the question will proceed, first by sketching briefly the world view from within which particular claims are being brought forth for the approbation of sexually intimate homosexual unions; second, by addressing the possibility of homosexual marriage from within the developed notion of marriage; and third, by addressing the issue of sexual intimacy in homosexual friendship.

The arguments defending the possibility of homosexual marriage and homosexual unions are set within an intellectual matrix fashioned by a particular worldview in which nature dissolves in the presence of a radical egalitarianism and choice, in which sensual pleasure in itself is the controlling good, and in which a particular kind of naturalistic fallacy, to wit, because some people are in fact homosexual, homosexual activities are good, is permitted to operate without challenge.

Now, as a starting point in response, whatever the relationship between members of the same sex might be, it is not marriage. Marriage is a union—physical, emotional, and spiritual—formed between one man and one woman. This union of sexually differentiated persons,

differentiated as male and female, instantiates ontological completeness. It is a unity in being as well as a unity of purpose. The union
in being, which is marriage, can only be constituted by one man and
one woman. Marriage requires the complementarity of two specific
kinds of persons who in their very nature are mutually ordered to each
other. Marriage is a unity on the level of essence. While other types
of complementarity may be possible among human beings as types
of moral unions or unions of activity or purpose, the very nature of
marriage—its "to be"—requires a particular kind of complementarity to form its unique kind of union. The new reality, the marriage,
lasts as long as the partners live. This union provides a loving matrix
for the generation and nurturing of children. The union provides the
intimate stable relationship for the appropriate satisfaction of sexual
pleasures.

The possibility of forming a particular kind of physical union, as
well as a particular type of rational and spiritual union, is required for
marriage regardless of whether the physical union is ever actualized.
Human life is embodied; the body counts. The sexual organs of man
and woman are apt to form, to complete, a particular type of union.
A homosexual relationship cannot be a union as a physical union in
the manner in which marriage is a physical union. The possibility of
forming a particular kind of physical union is required for marriage
regardless of whether the physical union is ever actualized. Physical
contact and material contiguity are not sufficient to form this type
of union. It is impossible for the sexual organs of two men together
or two women together to constitute the particular physical union,
the possibility of which is required for marriage. Furthermore, it is
impossible for two men together or two women together to form
the particular kind of rational and spiritual union required for marriage.

There are at least three objections to the position developed here.
One objection maintains that the claims regarding the nature of marriage as a lifelong heterosexual union are simply claims embedded
within particular traditions; the second claim is that marriage is simply
a social construct fashioned by the will of autonomous human beings
to enhance their flourishing; and the third objection converges around
a set of ideas that (a) there exists a variety of sexual manifestations in

addition to male and female; (b) there exists many different kinds of complementarity between human beings—the sexual complementarity of male and female is just one instance of possible complementarity; (c) other complementarities must be recognized and other types of union must be acknowledged; and (d) where unity of purpose is accompanied by commitment and would be enhanced by sexual intimacy, it should be permitted.

In regard to the first objection, the nature of marriage as a lifelong heterosexual union is a traditional claim, but that does not mean that marriage thus understood cannot be the correct understanding or that marriage thus understood has no place outside a particular tradition. This understanding of the nature of marriage is affirmed in many traditions and has been affirmed over time. Its test as a correct understanding is whether or not marriage thus understood and lived contributes to integral human flourishing—both for individuals and for society. The answers to this test are to be found in the concrete data of human living. While insight into the data may be encumbered by the necessity of longevity of the study and the possibility of bias in the observer, there does seem to be ongoing, recurrent, and wide-spread affirmation of the essential role of marriage thus understood as the hinge institution in the flourishing of both individuals and society. Is it not a key sign for the validity of a tradition its capacity to facilitate human flourishing? To this point in time such evidence vis-à-vis homosexual unions is lacking. The characterization of male homosexual relationships as self-centered, transitory, and promiscuous appears more than anecdotal. The study of female homosexual unions, as does research in many female related issues, has been scant. While evidence seems lacking for the existence of committed, exclusive, lifelong homosexual unions, the lack of evidence may have its source in the, perhaps understandable, failure of those who live in these relationships to come forward and testify to their value. Or on the other hand there may be no such evidence.

In regard to the second objection, marriage is not a social construct. Marriage has a nature that is both real and rational. Marriage has essential properties which are manifested over time in the being and becoming of the marriage. In the delineation of the essential properties of marriage, human reason confronts an existing reality insight into whose nature may be gained more or less completely, but whose nature cannot be deconstructed and recreated by wish. While human beings are free to enter into marriage or not, human beings are not free to decide the nature of marriage. What is required for the study of the essential nature of marriage is an adequate epistemology which is capable of accomplishing a more complete metaphysics which guides the formulation of a proper ethics. Insight into the nature of marriage, just as insight into the nature of anything else, such as the nature of light as waves or particles, has developed over time. Insight into the nature of marriage, as well as insight into the nature of light, is guided by reason in its ongoing, recurrent, related, cumulative, corrective operations employed in every cognitional enterprise yielding results that are cumulative and progressive. This method moves from experience to inquiry to understanding to judgment and then back to experience. Reason moves from the *quid sit* question that initiates inquiry to the *an sit* question which demands verification and does not rest until verification is accomplished (Lonergan 1964). Neither the nature of marriage nor the nature of light has changed, although the critical understanding of each, barring bias and blunder, has increased over time.

In regard to the third objection, there may be occurrences of sexual differentiation other than male and female, but these have the appearance of aberration and disorder. Furthermore, there are manifestations of different kinds of human complementarities, however, these complementarities themselves have to be assessed and have to be actualized in appropriate unions which are suitable for human flourishing. Complementarities in music bring forth the symphony, complementarities in human learning make possible the university, complementarities in athletic skills spawn baseball, basketball, football, and field hockey teams. On the other hand, a unique set of complementarities spawned Fascism, another Communism, and another still a gang intent on robbing a bank. The former sets of complementarities are normally valued as ordered to human flourishing and assessed as good. The latter sets of complementarities are normally valued as disordered and assessed as evil. The linkage claimed between the enhancement of committed sexual relationships and sexual intimacy has neither been established nor have defensible relationship limits been defined.

When sexual intimacy becomes considered as simply a more intense form of affection limited to those in special committed relationships, it becomes difficult to sustain defensible prohibitions of such intense affection in other important relationships such as student/teacher, physician/patient, trainer/athlete, parent/child.

Is it appropriate for two homosexual people to form a union of friendship? Yes, but remember true friendship is based not on pleasure or utility but on virtue. Should this particular kind of friendship include the satisfaction of sexual desires for reasons of enhancing the union of friendship? If, as a matter of fact, homosexual desires or inclinations are disordered, no. The actualization of disordered desires or inclinations corrupts the character of the person. This corruption affects the human being in two ways: (i) the satisfaction of the disordered passion reinforces or strengthens that particular passion which habituates the person in a particular direction, thus determining disordering of character and (ii) powerful passions can override and interfere with the development of other potentialities appropriate for integrated human life. Possible consequences for the individual are the interference with the attainment of the rational and transcendental ends of human life. This corruption of character has social consequences, which cannot fail to have an impact on the individual person, the friendship, and on the common good. This corruption of character has eternal consequences. It places at risk the love of God. A true friend does not desire the destruction of a friend. True and deep friendship is possible without sexual intimacy. To require sexual activity as a necessary enhancement of friendship is to have a narrow vision of the person, an impoverished understanding of friendship, and to give sex primacy over the person.

Should the friendship between homosexual persons include the type of intimate sexual activity reserved for marriage? No, and for several reasons. First, while genital stimulation is possible within a homosexual relationship, conjugal intercourse is not possible. Second, self-gratification rather than self-donation appears to be the end of intimate sexual activity outside of marriage whether that activity be engaged in by heterosexual persons or homosexual persons. Third, to seek sensual pleasure for its own sake is to engage in a particular type of hedonism. Further, pleasures are differentiated as appropriate or inappropriate—a distinction as old as at least the *Nicomachean Ethics* of Aristotle. Appropriate pleasure accompanies an act of human flourishing; it is the delight that is attendant to activities which accomplish human goods. Pleasures are designated good or evil following the kinds of activities that pleasures complete. And finally, the intimate sexual activity of conjugal intercourse is reserved to those who are married. Its pleasures facilitate the accomplishment of the multiple goods of marriage. It is an activity inappropriate to those who, whether they are heterosexual or homosexual, are not married.

The argument that homosexuality may have a material basis, as distinguished from situational and psychological homosexuality, in some persons does not salvage the defense of the possibility of homosexual marriage. There are other characteristics found in human beings that have a material basis, but no one presses the argument that social structures should be put in place for their actualization. For example, the claim has been made that the XYY chromosomal configuration found in some males, along with some other characteristics, appears to dispose them to violence. Society does not fashion structures for these males to satisfy their violent drives. Instead, society attempts to protect both society and these individuals from their violent proclivities. Schizophrenia and manic depression appear to have material bases in the brain. Nonetheless, they are still recognized as disorders and those who suffer these disorders are recognized as disabled and in need of help. So while schizophrenia, manic depression, double Y chromosome, and some forms of homosexuality may naturally occur in some individuals, these disordered inclinations are not natural to human beings as human beings. This distinction was made clearly by Thomas Aquinas in the following:

> For it happens in an individual that some one of the natural principles of the species is corrupted, so that something which is contrary to the specific nature, becomes accidentally natural to this individual … Consequently it happens that something which is not natural to man, either in regard to reason, or in regard to the preservation of the body, becomes connatural to this individual man, on account of their being some corruption of nature in him. And this corruption may be either on the part of the body,—from some ailment; thus to a man suffering from a fever, sweet things seem bitter, and

vice versa,—or from an evil temperament; thus some take pleasure in eating earth and coals and the like; or on the part of the soul; thus from the custom some take pleasure in cannibalism or in the unnatural intercourse of man and beast, or other such like things which are not in accord with human nature (Aquinas, *Summa theologiae* I-II, q. 31, a. 7).

Toward Completion

From the Theoretical to the Practical

Marriage as a Human Reality: As a human reality marriage has many goods to be accomplished—the goods of the marital union, the goods of children, and the goods of the individual partners including their sexual satisfaction. The marriage act is most complete when it instantiates all those goods in a single act, that is when the marriage act instantiates the union between loving spouses so that their act of conjugal intercourse (1) actualizes the personal union of husband and wife in such a way as to bring about the mutual sanctification of both, (2) is open to the possibility of the good of children—both *esse* and *bene esse*, and (3) is mutually satisfying for both husband and wife. Spouses ought to aspire to this reality and their consent to the vocation of marriage places the couple under obligation to achieve this reality. Marriage should be animated by the sacrificial spirit of Christ and the creative love of God. There exists then a presumption that to consent to marital intercourse is to intend all the goods of marriage.

However, in the real world of imperfect human beings the human response in imitation of the sacrificial and creative love of God remains finite, hence that response can be only that of which a finite and fallen being is capable. Moreover, there are sometimes serious reasons which override the presumption in favor of actualizing all the ends of marriage. Nonetheless, the reason must never be a response that is motivated by selfishness, the desire for luxury, or the sake of convenience.

The consequences of this more complete understanding of the nature of marriage and its ends as this understanding governs the reproductive finality are as follows. First, the judgment that the circumstances of a particular marriage require that reproduction be avoided is to be the prudential judgment of the marriage partners. The accomplishment of the intrinsic-contingent end of children as a horizontal finality is contrary to reasonable and responsible parenthood unless the conditions exist for the possibility of the emergence for the child of the higher levels of finality. Reasonable means, including abstinence, natural family planning, non-abortifacient contraceptives, and even—though rarely—sterilization, may be utilized, for a determinate or an indeterminate time, to prevent procreation within particular acts of conjugal intercourse within the vocation of marriage. Second, the judgment that the circumstances of a particular marriage require that artificial means, including homologous artificial insemination or homologous in *vitro* fertilization and embryo transfer, be utilized in order that reproduction be accomplished is to be the prudential judgment of the marriage partners. In the presence of defects in the physical system that serves to accomplish the reproductive end on the level of horizontal finality and in the presence of conditions in the marriage that are conducive to the emergence for the offspring of the higher levels of finality, reasonable means may be used to accomplish procreation. These reasonable means must respect the dignity of the marriage and the dignity of the human beings whose life is begun. Respect for the dignity of the new being requires, at a minimum, protection of life and protection from non-therapeutic experimentation.

There are several dangers to be avoided both in the matter of avoiding reproduction and in the matter of accomplishing reproduction. The first danger has it source in the fact that prudence, practical wisdom, if accomplished at all, is a rather late accomplishment in life. Some possible remedies for the lack of prudence are to have the counsel of wise men and women, married and unmarried, lay and religious; to have spiritual direction; to have frequent recourse to the sacraments; to pray and to study and to play together. In the matter of contraception, the couple must avoid developing a contraceptive mentality, that is, a fixed and powerful resolve that closes the marriage to the good of procreation in such a fashion that abortion becomes an acceptable remedy to failed contraception. In the too easy acceptance of pharmaceutical and mechanical contraception, lies the risk that the good of abstinence and the good of natural family planning may be ignored. Periodic abstinence and natural family planning provide husband and wife an opportunity to learn and to respond to the sexual rhythms, needs, and desires of each other. They learn to deal with these rhythms, needs, and desires in a distinctly human way—by a rational choice. The use of non-abortifacient chemical and physical contraceptives is not without risk to marriage. Among the possible dangers are the possibility of objectification of the wife by the husband and the lowering of the desire of the wife for her husband. In the matter of accomplishing the reproductive finality by the use of technological means there lie risks to both the marriage and the new human being. Children must be conceived from within the body of the marriage. There must be no third party material assistance whether or germ material or place of maturation. The intimacy of the marriage, of necessity, becomes open to the presence of technicians and scientists who have the expertise to assist the couple to attain the good of procreation. Couples must be aware of this intrusion and take appropriate means necessary to protect their intimacy and each other. Technicians and scientists who will assist the couple must be sensitive

Afterword

What is Christian marriage? This question confronts the Roman Catholic Church at the same time that the existence of marriage is under threat in the secular world. Closely related problems about morally permissive reproductive technology are no less controversial in and out of the Church. After reading Margaret Monahan Hogan's reissued book *Finality and Marriage* we can gain insight into where Catholics have come from, where we are now and where we may be going with these disputed questions.

I am grateful for Hogan's careful comprehensive scholarly examination of the relevant Church documents. Like many other Catholics I had read the encyclicals and letters but I did not have the resources for such a detailed and in depth treatment of traditional Catholic teachings as Hogan offers. Here we find explicated the influence of Aristotle, Augustine and Thomas Aquinas upon modern church statements. These philosophical reflections give a good workout for non-philosophical readers. The guiding influence of the modern philosopher Lonergan also shapes Hogan's analysis and gives those unfamiliar with his thought a sense of his approach to the practice of philosophy.

Through analysis of the documents Hogan presents a story of development and change in the Church's views of Christian marriage. Slowly, the historically conditioned elements in the concepts of marriage are being identified and isolated from what Hogan holds up as the positive permanent elements of the Catholic heritage. Evolution of doctrine comes from changes in ethical insight, changes in scientific knowledge and changes in the understanding of the nature of the marriage relationship. In particular the prejudice and negative bias against sexual intercourse gives way to a positive evaluation.

The growth of a view of marriage as a personalist procreative union is delineated. Hogan holds that when the understanding of marriage as a personal union of love becomes the controlling point of view, then changes in past and present church teachings become inevitable. A personalist unitive appreciation of marriage as a sacramental bond and lifelong relationship must become combined with a principle of totality in which parts must serve the whole. Moreover, when it is understood from biology that actual procreation takes place at a distance in time and space from the act of intercourse, then the requirement that each marital act of intercourse be inseparably unitive and procreative appears unwarranted. The bond is necessary in marriage but the goods of reproduction and fertility are contingent and probable. Childbearing may not be biologically possible or even a reasonable and responsible course of action in certain circumstances. Thus, Hogan morally accepts non-abortifacient contraception, sterilization and some forms of artificial reproductive technology that serve the good of marriage as a whole intimate personal union in Christ.

Anyone who analyzes development in the tradition and defends certain changes in Church teaching also has to argue for a positive view of evolution of doctrine. Hogan does this admirably in her newly added epilogue, citing Newman and the work of John Noonan. She recognizes that sometimes change can be a decline, but provides a solid foundation for her positive assessment of the move toward a personalist embodied unique marital union If you ever wanted to know why the arguments for the inseparability of procreation and unity in each conjugal act fail, this is the essay to read. The prudent acceptance of the options of contraception, sterilization and some reproductive technology are here defended as essential to a more complete Christian understanding of marriage. Yes, says Hogan, there are dangers to be avoided in the matter of avoiding reproduction or in accomplishing reproduction but this is true of every serious moral decision. I appreciate the way that in this work the tradition is appreciated, yet criticized and moved forward in an integrated way. No baby is thrown out with the bath water here!

As for the future, Hogan excludes the claims for accepting homosexual marriage. She grounds her position on her view of gender, embodied unity and the intrinsic nature of marriage as between a man and a woman. Even if one does not agree with this part of her argument, it is grounded in her defense of the unique dignity of marriage in the Christian tradition. Hogan claims that practical repercussions will follow from changes in philosophy and theology and I agree with her.

Having the church defend marriage as a good and uniquely challenging vocation will help real people in their daily lives.

Marriage is a demanding vocation because so many goods are involved. Partners must seek the good of the marriage, the good of existing children and the personal fulfillment of the individual partners. To live out such a call to love demands growth in character and holiness. For Hogan there is no going back to a narrower less demanding understanding of marriage as a personal union in Christ. An "incomplete understanding of the role of intercourse in marriage and a disordered understanding of the place of reproductive finality within marriage" had to evolve toward a more complete and Christian fullness. As with every doctrinal development and change that is defended, the analysis must show that it is more conforming to God's nature and the whole truth of Christian revelation. Hogan meets this test admirably.

Sidney Callahan, Ph.D.

Bibliography
Primary Sources

Aristotle. *Nicomachean Ethics. The Basic Works of Aristotle.* Ed. Richard McKeon. New York: Random House, Inc., 1941a.

―――. *Politics. The Basic Works of Aristotle.* Ed. Richard McKeon. New York: Random House, Inc., 1941b.

Augustine. *The Good of Marriage.* Tr. Charles T. Wilcox, M.M. In *Writings of Saint Augustine.* Edited by Roy J. Deferrari. New York: Fathers of the Church, 1955.

Davitt, Thomas E. *The Basic Values in Law.* Milwaukee: Marquette UP, 1978.

Doms, Herbert. *The Meaning and End of Marriage.* New York: Sheed and Ward, 1939.

[*Donum vitae.*] Congregation for the Doctrine of the Faith. *Instruction on Respect for Human Life in its Origin and on the Dignity of Procreation.* Boston: Daughters of Saint Paul, 1981.

von Hildebrand, Dietrich. *Marriage.* London: Longmans, Green and Co., 1942.

John Paul II. *The Role of the Christian Family in the Modern World. Familiaris consortio.* Boston: Daughters of Saint Paul, 1981.

John Paul II. *Evangelium vitae.* ORIGINS. April 6, 1995. Vol. 24, No. 42.

Lonergan, S.J., Bernard J.F. *Insight: A Study of Human Understanding.* New York: Philosophical Library Inc., 1964.

―――. *Method in Theology.* New York: Herder and Herder, 1972.

―――. "Dimensions of Meaning." *Collection.* Ed. F.E. Crowe, S.J. New York: Herder and Herder, 1967.

Majority Report. Pontifical Commission for the Study of the Problems of Population, Family and Births. "National Catholic Reporter." April 19, 1967.

Newman, John Henry. *An Essay on Development of Christian Doctrine.* Ed. Charles Frederick Harrold. New York: Longmans, Green and Co., 1949.

Paul VI. *Humanae vitae.* Acta Apostolicae Sedis. Vaticanis: Typis Polyglottis, 60: 481.

Pius XI. *Casti connubii.* New York: The Missionary Society of Saint Paul the Apostle, 1941.

Pius XII. *Sentence of the Holy Roman Rota.* Acta Apostolicae Sedis. Vaticanis: Typis Polyglottis, 36:179-200, 1944.

————. *Address to the Midwives.* Acta Apostolicae Sedis. Vaticanis: Typis Polyglottis, 43: 835-54, 1951a.

————. *Address to the Association of Large Families and the Family Front.* Acta Apostolicae Sedis. Vaticanis: Typis Polyglottis, 43: 855-60, 1951b.

————. *Address to the First International Congress on the Histopathology of the Nervous System.* Acta Apostolicae Sedis. Vaticanis: Typis Polyglottis, 44: 779-89, 1952.

————. *Address to the Twenty-Sixth Congress of the Italian Society of Urologists.* Acta Apostolicae Sedis. Vaticanis: Typis Polyglottis, 45: 673-79, 1954.

————. *Address to the Second World Congress on Fertility and Sterility.* Acta Apostolicae Sedis. Vaticanis: Typis Polyglottis, 48: 467-74, 1956.

————. *Address to the Seventh International Congress of Hematology.* Acta Apostolicae Sedis. Vaticanis: Typis Polyglottis, 50: 732-40, 1958a.

————. *Address to the Tenth National Congress of the Italian Society of Plastic Surgery.* Acta Apostolicae Sedis. Vaticanis: Typis Polyglottis, 50: 952-61, 1958b.

Rahner, Karl. "Marriage as a Sacrament." In *Theological Investigations X.* Tr. David Burke. New York: Herder and Herder, 1979.

Second Vatican Council. *Gaudium et spes. Pastoral Constitution on the Church in the Modern World.* Acta Apostolicae Sedis. Vaticanis: Typis Polyglottis, 58: 1067-1074, 1967.

————. *Dei verbum, Constitutiones,* Acta Apostolicae Sedis. Vaticanis: Typis Polyglottis, 430, 1967.

Synod of Bishops. *The Role of the Christian Family in the Modern World.* Washington: United States Catholic Conference, 1979.

Thomas Aquinas. *Summa theologiae. Basic Writings of St. Thomas Aquinas.* Edited by Anton C. Pegis. New York: Random House, 1944.

———. *De veritate.* V. III. Tr. R. W. Schmidt. Chicago: Henry Regnery Co., 1954.

———. *Summa contra gentiles.* Tr. English Dominican Fathers. New York: Benziger Brothers, 1923.

Wojtyla, Karol. *Love and Responsibility.* New York: Farrar, Straus and Giroux, Inc., 1981.

Secondary Sources

Anscombe, Elizabeth. "Contraception and Chastity." London: Catholic Truth Society, 1980.

Baron, Robert A. *Psychology: The Essential Science.* Boston: Allyn and Bacon, 1989.

Baum, O.S.A., Gregory and Donald Campion, S. J., *Commentary on De ecclesia in mundo huius temporis.* New York: Paulist Press, 1967.

Boyle, Joseph. "Marriage is an Institution Created by God: A Philosophical Analysis." *Proceedings of the American Catholic Philosophical Association*, 1989 pp. 2-15.

The Code of Canon Law. Canon Law Society of Great Britain and Ireland, in association with The Canon law Society of Australia and New Zealand and The Canadian Canon Law Society. The Code of Canon Law. Ann Arbor: William B. Eerdmans Publishing Company, 1983.

Cahill, Lisa Sowle. *Between the Sexes.* Philadelphia: Fortress Press, 1985.

Connery, S.J., John. Address to the Medical/Morals Commission of the Diocese of Green Bay, October 6, 1982 (unpublished).

———. "Notes on Moral Theology," *Theological Studies* 15: 1954 pp. 602-32.

Finnis, John. *Natural Law and Natural Rights.* Oxford: Clarendon Press, 1980.

Grisez, Germain. *Contraception and the Natural Law.* Milwaukee: Bruce Publishing Co., 1964.

Kelly, S.J., Gerald. "Pope Pius XII and the Principle of Totality," *Theological Studies,* 16: 1955 pp. 373-96.

Laros Matthias. "Revolutionierung der Ehe," *Hochland* 27: 1930 pp. 193-207.

Lawler, Ronald, Joseph M. Boyle, & William E. May. *Catholic Sexual Ethics: A Summary, Explanation, & Defense.* Indiana: Our Sunday Visitor, Inc., 1985.

Lonergan, S. J., Bernard. "Finality, Love, Marriage," *Collection*. Ed. F.E. Crowe, S.J. New York: Herder and Herder, 1967.

Mackin, S.J., Theodore. *What Is Marriage?* New York: Paulist Press, 1982.

Maritain, Jacques. "Natural Law." *Saint Thomas Aquinas on Politics and Ethics*. Tr. and ed. Paul E. Sigmund. New York: W. W. Norton and Company, 1988.

Martelet, S.J., Gustave. "Pour mieux comprendre l'encyclique Humanae vitae," *Nouvelle Revue Theologique*, 90:1968.

McCormick, S.J., Richard A. *How Brave A New World*. Washington: Georgetown U P, 1982.

———. *The Critical Calling*. Washington: Georgetown U P, 1989.

———. *Notes on Moral Theology 1965-1980*. Washington: University Press of America, 1981.

Muggeridge, Malcolm. "On *Humanae vitae*." New York: The National Committee of Catholic Laymen, Inc., 1980.

Noonan, John T. *Contraception: a History of its Treatment by the Catholic Theologians and Canonists*. Cambridge: Harvard UP, 1986.

———. "Development in Moral Doctrine." *Theological Studies*. 1993, pp. 662-77.

———. "On the Development of Doctrine." *America*, 1999, pp. 4-6.

Pellegrino, Edmund D., John Collins Harvey, John P. Langan. *Gift of Life*. Washington: Georgetown UP, 1990.

Pinckaers, O. P., Servais. *The Splendor of the Christian Life*. Tr. Michael Sherwin, O.P. Chicago: Saint Augustine Press, 2000.

Porter, O.P., Lawrence B. "*Humanae vitae*. A Decade Later: The Theologian behind the Encyclical." *Thomist*, 42: 1978, pp. 464-509.

Saxton, Stanley L., Patricia Voydanoff, Angela Ann Zukowski. *The Changing Family: Reflections on Familiaris consortio*. Chicago: Loyola U P, 1984.

Selling, Joseph A. "Moral Teaching, Traditional Teaching and Humanae vitae," *Louvain Studies*, 7: 1978, pp. 24-44.

Shannon, Thomas A. and Lisa Sowle Cahill. *Religion and Artificial Reproduction*. New York: Crossroad, 1988.

Smith, Henry Ignatius. *Classification of Desires in Saint Thomas and in Modern Sociology*. Washington: National Catholic Press, 1915.

Index

About the author

Margaret Monahan Hogan is the Chairperson of the Philosophy Department at King's College. She was the founding
Director of King's College Center for Ethics and Public Life. In

1999-2000, she was a senior visiting fellow
at the Notre Dame Center for Ethics and
Public Life and served on the Advisory Board
of the Notre Dame Center for Ethics and
Culture. She has served on the Independent
Review Board for the Diocese of Scranton
since 1993. The review board oversees clergy
sexual misconduct.

Dr. Hogan served as President of the Center for Academic
Integrity, which has its home at Duke University, in 2001 and
2002. She also serves as medical ethicist to the Wyoming Val-
ley Health Care System and to the Allied Services Health Care
System.

She has just been named to the McNerney-Hanson Chair in
Ethics at the University of Portland in Oregon. She is the first
recipient to be awarded the chair, which includes appointment
as full professor with tenure in the Philosophy Department at
Portland.

She and her husband Tom are the parents of six children.